Minnesota

Wisconsin

Michigan

Iowa

Illinois

Indiana

Ohio

Pennsylvania

New York

Maine

VT.

N.H.

MASS.

R.I.

CONN.

New
Jersey

DEL.

MD.

West
Virginia

Virginia

Missouri

Kentucky

North
Carolina

Tennessee

Arkansas

South
Carolina

Mississippi

Alabama

Georgia

Louisiana

Florida

The Spirit
of America

The Spirit
of America

The Spirit of America

A STATE-BY-STATE CELEBRATION

CHARLES MATHES

Introduction by
Bob Hope

GALLERY BOOKS
An Imprint of W. H. Smith Publishers Inc.
112 Madison Avenue
New York City 10016

GALLERY BOOKS
An Imprint of W. H. Smith Publishers Inc.
112 Madison Avenue
New York City 10016

An M & M Book

Copyright 1990 by Moore & Moore Publishing

ISBN 0 8317 0353 9

The Spirit of America **was prepared and produced by Moore & Moore Publishing, 11 W. 19th Street, New York, N.Y. 10011**

Project Director & Editor: Gary Fishgall

Photo Research: David Blankenship

Senior Editorial Assistant: Shirley Vierheller; Editorial Assistants: David Blankenship, Ben D'Amprisi, Jr., Maxine Dormer, Sarah Boyer; Copy Editing: Bert N. Zelman and Keith K. Walsh of Publishers Workshop, Inc.

Designer: Binns & Lubin

Separations and Printing: Regent Publishing Services Ltd.

Typesetting: Village Type & Graphics

This edition was published in 1990 by Gallery Books, an imprint of W.H. Smith Publishers, Inc. 112 Madison Avenue, New York, New York 10016

First Published in the United States

Gallery Books are available for bulk purchase for sales promotions and premium use. For details write or telephone the Manager of Special Sales, W.H. Smith Publishers, Inc., 112 Madison Avenue, New York, New York 10016. (212) 532-6600

Contents

Preceding pages: Statue of Liberty, New York City
These pages: Sea World of Texas, San Antonio

Introduction

I consider myself a pretty lucky guy. I've been blessed with a wonderful family, good friends and the ability to make people all over the world laugh. All I have to do is demonstrate my golf swing. But I think that the luckiest break I've had in my life is to be an American.

You know, Americans are a unique breed of people. We came out of every background and tradition you can name to make this great land our home. There are 50 states now—up from 13 when I was a boy—and each has its own unique spirit. Over the years I've had the privilege of visiting them all and, believe me when I tell you, no two are alike. From East Coast skyscrapers to the industrial heartland, from Southern hospitality to California dreamin', from the warmth of Hawaii to the cold of Alaska, this is one beautiful country.

The folks who live in our United States are as different as the terrain. There are farmers and astronauts, mechanics and teachers, salesmen and cowboys, doctors, lawyers and Indian chiefs, actors and even comedians. You can't name a character trait that somebody here doesn't have or a way to cook a chicken that someone hasn't tried. The funny thing is, though, no matter how different we are, we have one thing in common. We're all Americans.

Early in my career while playing the vaudeville circuit, I found myself in a strange town with only one quarter between me and starvation. I stared at the quarter trying to decide whether to buy coffee and doughnuts and a room for the night or purchase a bus ticket back to Cleveland. I looked at that quarter a long time and memorized everything on it—most notably the motto "E Pluribus Unum"—which, with my limited knowledge of Latin, I understood to mean—"one out of many."

Then I saw that 'unum' came at the end of the motto and I suddenly read the words in a new way, "Out of many, one." That's when I realized what this country is all about. It's many people, many states, many traditions united into one—and that the whole nation was greater than the sum of its parts. I might be alone and broke, but I belonged. I was part of a larger picture, an equal part. I was an American. And there was something else on that quarter which is terribly important—the words, "In God We Trust." We trust in God. We count our blessings. We keep going.

What did I do with the quarter? I had doughnuts and coffee, took a room for the night and called my agent. (You could do all that for a quarter in those days.)

This book is about the different spirit of each state. Every one of them has its own special style, its own customs, its own food and scenic attractions. When you add up all the differences, however, you're left with one common heritage—America. E Pluribus Unum. We may be fifty states and two hundred fifty million people, but we're one nation . . . and I'm proud to be a part of it.

CAPTAIN JOHN SMITH MONUMENT, JAMESTOWN, VIRGINIA

CROTON, VERMONT

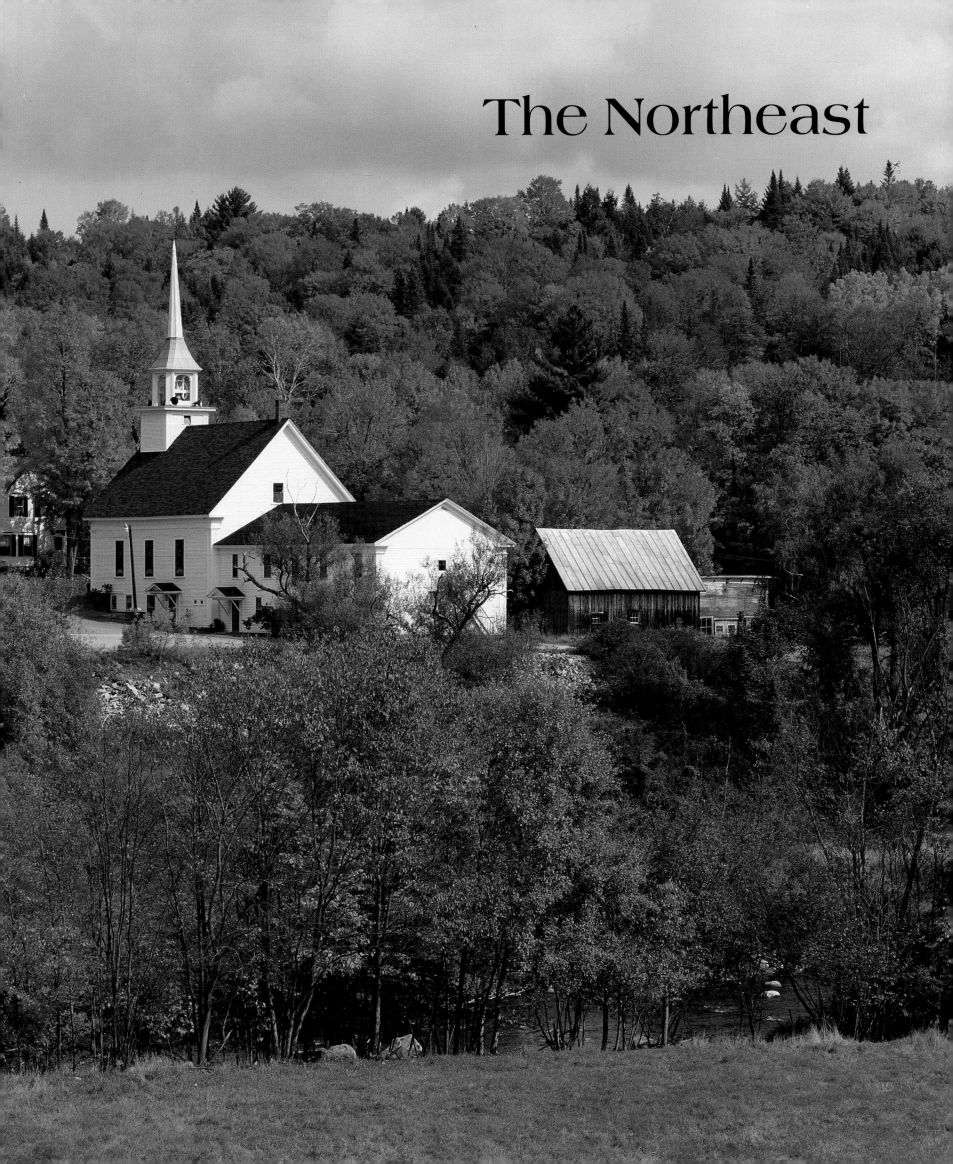

The Northeast

Maine

THE PINE TREE STATE

Waves crashing on a rocky shore, a moose drinking from a crystal lake, mountain pine trees, light-houses and fishing towns, windjammers and white beaches—Maine offers the kind of pictures you usually only see on postcards.

Nearly 90 percent of the state is forest, the largest wilderness east of the Mississippi River and one of the world's largest pulp paper producers. The state also grows 98 percent of America's lowbush blueberries and is third in potato production.

Maine's large cities, led by Portland, are thriving with new business and reconstruction, but it is the small towns and seaports that give the state its unique character. There is Blue Hill with her pottery shops, artist retreats like Wiscasset and Belfast, the popular boating communities of Boothbay, the classic New England village of Bethel, and jewel-like Camden with her harbor full of tall-masted schooners and yachts.

Ogunquit lives up to the meaning of its Indian name, "beautiful place by the sea." In Eastport the tides are the highest in the country (20–28 feet) and its residents are the first in America to see the rising sun. The Fryeburg Fair is over 135 years old and offers everything from record-breaking hogs to award-winning Christmas trees. Bar Harbor, long the retreat of the wealthy, is the gateway to Acacia National Park, the only national park in the Northeast. Four million visitors each year come to see its spectacular cliffs, crags, and coves.

As if "Vacationland" didn't say it all, a lobster has now been added to Maine's license plate, thanks to the lobbying efforts of a bunch of crusty Down-Easters who took time out from elementary school just to sign petitions!

PORTLAND HEAD LIGHTHOUSE, PORTLAND

ORIGIN OF NAME
To distinguish the mainland from
the offshore islands; may also refer
to the French province of Mayne,
owned by Charles I's wife

CAPITAL
Augusta

STATE FLOWER
White Pine Cone and Tassel

STATE BIRD
Chickadee

YEAR OF STATEHOOD
1820 (23rd state)

FAMOUS DOWN-EASTERS
James G. Blaine, Hannibal Hamlin,
Henry Wadsworth Longfellow, Edna
St. Vincent Millay, Kate Douglas
Wiggin

PORTLAND

ACADIA NATIONAL PARK, BAR HARBOR

SHEEPSCOT

COMMON GROUND COUNTRY FAIR, WINDSOR

14

Hot or Cold Boiled
LOBSTER
(BUTTER 50¢)

★ ROY MOORE LOBSTER
WHOLESALE · est. 1918 · RET

- OPEN

Delaware

THE FIRST STATE
THE DIAMOND STATE

Settled by Swedes, conquered by Dutchmen, seized by the English, then ceded to Pennsylvania, Delaware was the first state to ratify the U.S. Constitution. Today it is the "Corporate Capital of the World," home to nearly 200,000 corporations, including half the Fortune 500.

Though only 96 miles long and 9 to 35 miles wide, Delaware is a huge chemical and poultry center (Sussex County produces more broiler chickens than any other county in the nation), and also boasts world-famous museums, unspoiled beaches, picture-postcard towns, and gentle farmlands.

Wilmington, ideally located halfway between New York and Washington, is full of legacies from the du Pont family, a name that has been linked with the state ever since a Frenchman named Eleuthère Irénée du Pont built a gunpowder mill on the banks of the Brandywine River. Perhaps the most famous bequest is the spectacular Winterthur Museum and Gardens—the world's premier collection of American decorative arts from 1640 to 1840.

The cobblestone streets of New Castle, site of William Penn's first landing in America, date from Colonial times, and the town square looks much as it did then. Dover, the state capital, brims with Victorian gingerbread homes and historic buildings on the town green. Rehoboth Beach was originally the home of Methodist camp meetings (the word "rehoboth" is Biblical in origin, meaning "room enough"). Now so many politicians and lawmakers from Washington, D.C., vacation here that it is often referred to as the nation's summer capital.

And, finally, in case you thought Delaware's favorable business climate is only geared to rich corporations, shopping there might change your mind. There's no sales tax.

ORIGIN OF NAME
For Thomas West, Baron De La Warr, an early governor of Virginia

CAPITAL
Dover

STATE FLOWER
Peach Blossom

STATE BIRD
Blue Hen Chicken

YEAR OF STATEHOOD
1787 (1st state)

FAMOUS DELAWAREANS
Thomas F. Bayard, Henry Seidel Canby, E. I. du Pont, John P. Marquand, Howard Pyle, Caesar Rodney

ELMER'S MARKET, SOUTHERN DELAWARE

RODNEY SQUARE, WILMINGTON

GARRISON LAKE, SMYRNA

WINTERTHUR MUSEUM AND GARDENS, WINTERTHUR

17

Half the population of Ohio can be found in the metropolitan areas of the three C's—Cleveland, Cincinnati, and Columbus—which, with cities like Akron, Toledo, and Youngstown, make the state one of the nation's industrial leaders.

Not all of Ohio is urbanized, however. Verdant countryside, dairylands, pastures, farming communities, and villages that look like they were plucked from New England cover the state.

Great art museums, theater, and dance can be found here, as well as top sports teams (the Pro Football Hall of Fame is in Canton), Indian mounds, and the largest Amish population in the world. It's a wholesome place. The official state drink is tomato juice. The official insect is the ladybug.

Ohio has produced seven presidents (all Republicans), but according to *The Old Farmer's Almanac*, it is also the home of the disposable diaper, the world's largest cuckoo clock, the world's largest lawnmower, the farthest chicken flight and longest gourd, the towns of Fizzleville, Knockemstiff, and Pee Pee, the last surviving soldier of the American Revolution, the last passenger pigeon, the first aluminum saucepan, and the place where Life Savers™, Crisco™, and the phrase "rock 'n' roll" all came from.

But Ohio doesn't look backward. After all, this is the state where the Wright Brothers built their flying machine in a Dayton bicycle shop, where astronauts John Glenn and Neil Armstrong grew up dreaming of the stars. Even now Ohio is rebuilding its aging cities and again looking to the future.

Ohio

THE BUCKEYE STATE

CINCINNATI

19

THE CINCINNATI BENGALS

THE JAMES A. GARFIELD MONUMENT, CLEVELAND

THE WESTSIDE MARKET, CLEVELAND

THE UNION TERMINAL, CINCINNATI

ORIGIN OF NAME
From an Iroquois word meaning the "beautiful river"

CAPITAL
Columbus

STATE FLOWER
Scarlet Carnation

STATE BIRD
Cardinal

YEAR OF STATEHOOD
1803 (17th state)

FAMOUS OHIOANS
Clarence Darrow, Clark Gable, Bob Hope, Jack Nicklaus, Jesse Owens, John D. Rockefeller, Harriet Beecher Stowe, James Thurber

THE CLEVELAND ARCADE

APOLLO 15, THE U.S. AIR FORCE MUSEUM, DAYTON

MAPLE SUGARING, CABOT

The famous Green Mountains, Vermont's spine, are lush and inviting in summer, snow white in winter, and for a short few weeks in the fall, aflame with impossible brilliance, a rainbow of foliage, a riot of color.

Killington, Sugarbush, Stowe—some of the best skiing in the East can be found in this independent state, the least crowded in New England. Burlington, on beautiful Lake Champlain, is the only town with a population of more than 25,000. Nearly twice as many people work in New York's Empire State Building than live in Montpelier, which, with only 8000 residents, is the smallest state capital in the country. Even an industrial center like Bennington, once Ethan Allen's home base (the Green Mountain Boys were also known as the Bennington Mob), seems a natural place to find the world's largest collection of Grandma Moses's paintings.

When the snow melts, Vermonters tap the sugar maples (producing more syrup than anywhere else in America), work the quarries and mines (Vermont leads the nation in granite and marble production), and manufacture everything from furniture to fishing rods year round. Although many of our impressions of Vermont are pastoral, and in fact there are more dairy cows per capita here than anywhere else in America, only 7 percent of the population makes its living in agriculture. But from cheddar cheese to Ben and Jerry's™ ice cream, what Vermonters do produce, they produce with a unique Yankee style.

For instance, take that famous Vermont product, Calvin Coolidge, 30th President of the United States. When asked what a clergyman had said in a sermon about sin, old Silent Cal replied, "He was against it."

INDEPENDENCE DAY PARADE, BARTON

ORIGIN OF NAME
From the French *vert mont*, which means "green mountain"

CAPITAL
Montpelier

STATE FLOWER
Red Clover

STATE BIRD
Hermit Thrush

YEAR OF STATEHOOD
1791 (14th state)

FAMOUS VERMONTERS
Ethan Allen, Chester A. Arthur, Orson Bean, Calvin Coolidge, Adm. George Dewey, John Dewey, Stephen A. Douglas, Jim Fisk

Vermont
THE GREEN MOUNTAIN STATE

23

Massachusetts

THE BAY STATE
THE OLD COLONY STATE

The snappy television commercials proclaim that "the Spirit of Massachusetts is the Spirit of America." With a history that includes the Pilgrims, Paul Revere's Ride, Lexington and Concord, and the Boston Tea Party, the state can't be accused of much exaggeration.

Practically every village and town in the state has some claim to fame. Gloucester is the country's oldest seaport and is still one of the world's leading fishing centers. Salem, another old maritime town, was where the infamous witch trials occurred and where Nathaniel Hawthorne wrote his books. The wide white beaches of Cape Cod and islands like Martha's Vineyard and Nantucket have beckoned to generations of Americans. In Plymouth at Plimoth Plantation, one of the nation's finest "living history museums," you can see what daily life was like for the Pilgrims, and Old Sturbridge Village offers a picture of an 1830s New England town. Towns like Lenox, Stockbridge, and Williamstown offer music, theater, and dance festivals each summer amid Berkshire Mountain scenery. Lowell, Lawrence, Springfield, Worcester, and scenic Fall River exemplify the state's industry and work ethic.

But it's Boston that ties it all together: Boston, the oldest major city in America (1630); Boston, with its famous Common, its historic Beacon Hill, its Freedom Trail, its fabulous museums; Boston, home of the MTA, the U.S.S. *Constitution* ("Old Ironsides"), Bunker Hill, and the Red Sox.

Over 400 institutions of higher learning are scattered around the city, but the most famous (and the country's oldest college) is Harvard. How do you get to Harvard? Study. And bring $18,000 to cover tuition.

OLD STURBRIDGE VILLAGE, STURBRIDGE

FANEUIL HALL MARKETPLACE, BOSTON

HARVARD UNIVERSITY, CAMBRIDGE

CRANBERRY HARVEST, PLYMOUTH

HANCOCK SHAKER VILLAGE, PITTSFIELD

GAY HEAD CLIFFS, MARTHA'S VINEYARD

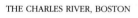

THE CHARLES RIVER, BOSTON

TRURO BEACH, CAPE COD

THE BOSTON POPS

THE OLD SOUTH MEETING HOUSE, BOSTON

THE MINUTEMAN STATUE, CONCORD

MASSACHUSETTS INSTITUTE OF TECHNOLOGY, CAMBRIDGE

BRANT POINT, NANTUCKET

ORIGIN OF NAME
In honor of Queen Henrietta Maria,
wife of England's Charles I

CAPITAL
Annapolis

STATE FLOWER
Black-Eyed Susan

STATE BIRD
Baltimore Oriole

YEAR OF STATEHOOD
1788 (7th state)

FAMOUS MARYLANDERS
Spiro Agnew, Eubie Blake, Francis
Scott Key, H. L. Mencken, William
Pinkney, "Babe" Ruth, Wallis Warfield
Simpson, Upton Sinclair

THE 132ND PENNSYLVANIA VOLUNTEER INFANTRY MONUMENT, ANTIETAM

THE WALTERS ART GALLERY, BALTIMORE

HARBOR PLACE, BALTIMORE

30

THE U.S. NAVAL ACADEMY, ANNAPOLIS

Maryland

Cradled by the bountiful waters of the Chesapeake Bay, Maryland has one of the longest waterfronts in America and proves it: you can't go anywhere in the state where they don't serve those famous Maryland crabs (usually with just some napkins and a wooden mallet so you can "pick them" yourself).

The birthplace of American railroading and site of the first telegram communication, Maryland enjoys as rich a history as it does a harvest.

Annapolis, the capital, a charming port city of narrow streets and Georgian architecture, was founded in 1649 by 10 Puritan families seeking freedom from religious persecution. It served as the nation's first peacetime capital (between November 1783 and August 1784) and, since 1845, has been the home of the U.S. Naval Academy.

Baltimore today is undergoing a rejuvenation, spurred by developments like Harborplace. The National Aquarium is here. So is the famous Peale Museum, the nation's oldest museum building. Everywhere, the city's past is being carefully preserved. In Baltimore's harbor you can still walk the deck of the U.S. frigate *Constellation*, the first commissioned ship of the U.S. Navy, or visit Fort McHenry, which the British bombarded in the War of 1812, inspiring Francis Scott Key to write "The Star-Spangled Banner."

The Civil War's bloodiest battle was fought in Maryland, at Antietam; Camp David has been the retreat of American presidents since Franklin D. Roosevelt (who called it Shangri-la); and you can still see the famous wild ponies on Assateague Island, whose ancestors swam ashore from a foundering Spanish galleon in the 16th century.

But of Maryland's many claims to fame, perhaps the most outstanding is her generosity: the land for Washington, D.C., was a gift from Maryland to the nation in 1791.

OYSTERING, CHESAPEAKE BAY

THE NASA GODDARD VISITOR CENTER MUSEUM, GREENBELT

WILD FOWL

31

New York
THE EMPIRE STATE

New York City. The people in its 300 square miles outnumber the populations of North and South Dakota, Montana, Wyoming, Nevada, Idaho, Alaska, and Utah combined. It has more Italians than Rome, more Irish than Dublin, and more Jews than Jerusalem. Just the telephone wires under New York's pavements would stretch around the world 40 times with enough left over to get to the moon and back. Twice.

It's a town built on superlatives: great buildings, superb restaurants, fabulous shopping, unique museums, theaters, and music. No wonder 18 million visitors make New York City their destination each year, more than any other place in the world. In fact, to many people New York means the Big Apple, which is a pity since the Empire State has so much more to offer.

Take the lovely Finger Lakes, for instance, which stretch across the middle of the state like a welcoming hand and offer everything from wineries to glass-making. Or the resorts of Lake Placid and Lake George, nestled like jewels in the magnificent Adirondacks—more than 6 million acres of rugged beauty, the largest natural preserve in the East. The accent is on fishing and boating when you go to the Thousand Islands, dotting the St. Lawrence Seaway. The world's largest muskie (an ounce shy of 70 pounds) was landed here.

There are dozens of places in New York worth a look: historic Albany, with its capitol building and the Nelson Rockefeller Empire State Plaza; the quaint villages and resort towns of eastern Long Island; the industrial centers of Syracuse, Rochester, and Utica; the fabled resorts of the Catskills; and, of course, the honeymoon capital of the world, Niagara Falls.

What more can you say about a place with such an embarrassment of riches? The state offers its own, characteristically understated suggestion: "I Love New York!"

WOODSTOCK GENERAL STORE, WOODSTOCK

TIMES SQUARE, NEW YORK CITY

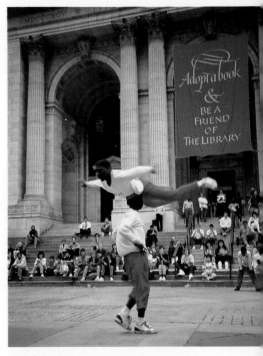

BREAK DANCERS IN FRONT OF THE NEW YORK
PUBLIC LIBRARY, NEW YORK CITY

NIAGARA FALLS

CENTRAL PARK, NEW YORK CITY

ORIGIN OF NAME
For England's Duke of York and
Albany, whose brother, Charles II,
granted him title to the territory

CAPITAL
Albany

STATE FLOWER
Rose

STATE BIRD
Bluebird

YEAR OF STATEHOOD
1788 (11th state)

FAMOUS NEW YORKERS
Susan B. Anthony, Henry and
William James, Herman Melville,
Franklin D. Roosevelt, Theodore
Roosevelt

THE EMPIRE STATE BUILDING, NEW YORK CITY

THE SARATOGA RACE TRACK

THE STOCK EXCHANGE, NEW YORK CITY

36

EMPIRE STATE PLAZA, ALBANY

THE U.S. MILITARY ACADEMY, WEST POINT

ALLEGHENY STATE PARK, SALAMANCA

FARM, NEAR HOOSICK FALLS

Little Rhode Island, the smallest state, has always been a giant in matters of conscience and religious freedom.

In 1636, Roger Williams, exiled by Massachusetts, founded Providence, where God's providence had led him. Later, Anne Hutchinson and her followers settled Portsmouth. In 1657, Quakers made Newport their first settlement in America, and Sephardic Jews from Holland arrived in the town the following year. Perhaps nothing illustrates Rhode Island's continuing freedom-loving spirit better than its pro-claiming its independence from England two months before the Declaration of Independence was signed.

Providence, Rhode Island's capital and financial center, is presently undergoing an urban redevelopment project so ambitious that rivers are being rerouted to their original courses. The city has the largest concentration of colonial homes in America and still keeps the street names its founder bestowed: Benefit, Friendship, and Hope.

Thanks to manufacturing and textile centers like Pawtucket and Woonsocket, Rhode Island's industry holds its own against far bigger states, but few cities in America can compete with Newport for glamor, history, and style.

Wealthy merchants summered in Newport as early as 1720, but it was during America's "Gilded Age" that this proud seaport became *the* resort for the rich and famous. Astors, Vanderbilts, Belmonts, the cream of society, built their summer "cottages" here by the shore —often 70-room replicas of European palaces. Today, many of the great houses are open to the public, who are more likely to have hit town for the restaurants, the music festivals, or even the International Tennis Hall of Fame than for "the season."

THE BREAKERS AND CLIFF WALK, NEWPORT

TUNA TOURNAMENT, BLOCK ISLAND SOUND

ORIGIN OF NAME
In 1524, Giovanni de Verrazano recorded sighting an island about the size of Rhodes, though the state may have been named "Roode Eylandt" by Dutch explorer Adrian Block because of its red clay

CAPITAL
Providence

STATE FLOWER
Violet

STATE BIRD
Rhode Island Red

YEAR OF STATEHOOD
1790 (13th state)

FAMOUS RHODE ISLANDERS
George M. Cohan, Nelson Eddy, Christopher and Oliver La Farge, Matthew C. and Oliver Perry, Gilbert Stuart

Rhode Island
THE OCEAN STATE

PROVIDENCE

MAXI WORLDS, NEWPORT

Seen from its turnpike, the most traveled road in America, New Jersey seems like one vast stretch of asphalt punctuated with smoke-stacks.

From the tree-lined streets and flower beds of Cape May, however, New Jersey looks like a Victorian postcard. There are towns such as Princeton and Lambertville, where the state seems quaint and charming, and those like Atlantic City and Wildwood, where it seems like a perpetual carnival. In the 1000 square miles of the Pine Barrens, New Jersey looks like a limitless, uninhabited marsh, while from the farms that make it one of the nation's top five producers of blueberries, cranberries, tomatoes, asparagus, and summer potatoes, New Jersey truly looks like the Garden State.

There's no denying, of course, that New Jersey is one of the most densely populated and industrialized states. It fairly bustles with oil refineries and factories.

Still, just outside of Trenton is the beautiful Washington Crossing State Park, where George Washington made his historic trip across the Delaware. The trend-setting Meadowlands Sports Complex and the fastest-growing airport in the country have injected new life into the Newark area. And the 127-mile Jersey Shore, one of the most valuable pieces of real estate in the world, offers everything from pristine beaches to top-notch museums to saltwater taffy. Captain Kidd's famous treasure may even be buried somewhere along Long Beach Island.

And, finally, it was from New Jersey's harbors that generations of immigrants caught their first glimpse of what America stands for. That's right—the Statue of Liberty and Ellis Island, are both located in New Jersey waters.

New Jersey
THE GARDEN STATE

DELAWARE WATER GAP NATIONAL RECREATION AREA, PENNSYLVANIA BORDER

PINK HOUSE, CAPE MAY

ATLANTIC CITY

JERSEY SHORE AT ISLAND BEACH

GREAT ADVENTURE, JACKSON

ORIGIN OF NAME
Named by Sir George Carteret, former Governor and defender of England's Isle of Jersey

CAPITAL
Trenton

STATE FLOWER
Purple Violet

STATE BIRD
Eastern Goldfinch

YEAR OF STATEHOOD
1787 (3rd state)

FAMOUS NEW JERSEYANS
Count Basie, James Fenimore Cooper, Stephen Crane, Thomas Edison, Joyce Kilmer, Paul Robeson, Frank Sinatra, Bruce Springsteen, Walt Whitman

THE MEADOWLANDS GRAND PRIX, EAST RUTHERFORD

PRINCETON UNIVERSITY, PRINCETON

THE BOARDWALK, ATLANTIC CITY

43

With its rugged landscapes, towering mountains, and elegant lakes, New Hampshire even looks like a place that would adopt the motto "Live Free or Die."

Abundant water power turned the state into a manufacturing center early in its history, and thanks to its proximity to Boston on the southeast, New Hampshire is now one of the nation's most industrialized states and New England's fastest growing.

Though there's an active Shaker community in Concord, historic homes and a bustling Navy Yard in the seacoast town of Portsmouth, and all manner of water sports on lakes like Sunapee and Winnipesaukee, New Hampshire nevertheless is still dominated by its majestic northern White Mountains.

There are 1100 unspoiled square miles in the White Mountains National Forest, and the scenery from resort towns like North Conway is breathtaking. In the Franconia Notch alone you can see the Flume (an 800-foot natural gorge), the famous stone profile in the rocks known as the "Old Man of the Mountains," and the first aerial tramway in North America. And driving the Kancamagus Highway is like being in the lap of God.

The 6288-foot Mount Washington in the 11-peak Presidential Range is the highest mountain in northeastern America. The world's first cog railway (1869) leads to its summit, where the highest wind speed in history (231 miles per hour) was recorded in 1934. Even though the average temperature at the top of Mount Washington is only 26.7 degrees Fahrenheit, the view is worth it. P. T. Barnum called it "the second greatest show on earth."

CRAFTS FAIR, MT. SUNAPEE STATE PARK, SUNAPEE

OLDE NUTFIELD, CHESTER

THE OLD COUNTRY STORE, MOULTONBORO CORNER

ORIGIN OF NAME
Named by Capt. John Mason, one of the founders of Portsmouth, after his home county in England

CAPITAL
Concord

STATE FLOWER
Purple Lilac

STATE BIRD
Purple Finch

YEAR OF STATEHOOD
1788 (9th state)

FAMOUS NEW HAMPSHIRITES
Salmon P. Chase, Mary Baker Eddy, Robert Frost, Horace Greeley, Augustus Saint-Gaudens, Daniel Webster

New Hampshire
THE GRANITE STATE

Pennsylvania
THE KEYSTONE STATE

America was invented in Pennsylvania.

Philadelphia is where the Declaration of Independence was signed and the U.S. Constitution was written, where the First Continental Congress met and where the Liberty Bell still rests. Philly also produced the country's first hospital, university, stock exchange, and zoo, and is still the place to go for great art, wonderful music, and cheese steaks.

But look at the rest of Pennsylvania: the quiet dignity of the battlefield at Gettysburg; the old steel town of Pittsburgh, being reborn in glass-sheathed towers; Hershey, where the streetlights are shaped like chocolate kisses and the smell of cocoa fills the air; Valley Forge, where Washington's army passed a cruel winter; the half-million acres of woodlands in the Allegheny National Forest; Bucks County, with its country inns and covered bridges; Lancaster County, where Amish farmers still drive horse-drawn buggies through the streets and where they serve all you can eat "family style"; the industrial bustle of cities like Easton, Scranton, Wilkes-Barre, and Allentown; the gorgeous Brandywine Valley, captured in paintings by generations of Wyeths; the heart-shaped swimming pools and honeymoon retreats of the Poconos.

With such incredible diversity, it would seem hard to find anything about this state that's truly surprising. Of course, you knew that the statue of William Penn on Philadelphia's City Hall is the largest single piece of sculpture on any building in the world, and that Lancaster, which gave the American pioneers the Conestoga wagon, was capital of the United States for one day, and that Pennsylvania grows more than 60 percent of the nation's mushrooms. . . .

PITTSBURGH

RITTENHOUSE SQUARE, PHILADELPHIA

47

FALLINGWATER, MILL RUN

BOAT HOUSE ROW, PHILADELPHIA

INDEPENDENCE NATIONAL HISTORIC PARK, PHILADELPHIA

THE BENJAMIN FRANKLIN PARKWAY AND CITY HALL, PHILADELPHIA

THE PHILADELPHIA 76ERS

THE FRANKLIN MEMORIAL, PHILADELPHIA

THE PHILADELPHIA MUSEUM OF ART

ORIGIN OF NAME
In honor of William Penn's father;
"sylvania" means woodland

CAPITAL
Harrisburg

STATE FLOWER
Mountain Laurel

STATE BIRD
Ruffed Grouse

YEAR OF STATEHOOD
1787 (2nd state)

FAMOUS PENNSYLVANIANS
Marian Anderson, Daniel Boone,
Andrew Carnegie, Stephen Foster,
Benjamin Franklin, Robert Fulton,
James Michener, Betsy Ross,
Andrew Wyeth

THE LIBERTY BELL, PHILADELPHIA

DELAWARE WATER GAP NATIONAL RECREATION AREA, NEW JERSEY BORDER

ECKLEY MINER'S VILLAGE, ECKLEY

Connecticut

THE NUTMEG STATE
THE CONSTITUTION STATE

PUTNAM MEMORIAL PARK, REDDING

MYSTIC SEAPORT, MYSTIC

YALE UNIVERSITY, NEW HAVEN

THE HARTFORD CIVIC CENTER

ORIGIN OF NAME
From an Indian word meaning
"beside the long tidal river"

CAPITAL
Hartford

STATE FLOWER
Mountain Laurel

STATE BIRD
American Robin

YEAR OF STATEHOOD
1788 (5th state)

FAMOUS "NUTMEGGERS"
P. T. Barnum, Samuel Colt, Nathan
Hale, Katharine Hepburn, J. P.
Morgan, Noah Webster, Eli Whitney

New England begins in this state of seaports and church steeples, bustling cities, and quiet towns.

In 1639, the English settlements of Wethersfield, Windsor, and Hartford united to form the Connecticut Colony, and adopted what is considered the world's first written constitution, the Fundamental Orders. Connecticut to this day keeps "The Constitution State" as its official nickname.

Pioneers of American enterprise like Eli Whitney, Samuel Colt, and Charles Goodyear helped Connecticut become one of the young nation's most industrialized states, and its factories still produce everything from pharmaceuticals to helicopters, silverware to submarines.

Helped by its proximity to New York City, Connecticut is the nation's wealthiest state in terms of per capita income. Hartford, the capital and the place where Mark Twain wrote *Adventures of Huckleberry Finn*, is also capital of the nation's insurance business and a model of successful urban renewal. Other important Connecticut cities include corporate and manufacturing centers like Stamford, Bridgeport, and New Haven, home of Yale University.

For pure enchantment, however, Connecticut's small towns offer unique delights. There's the Hitchcock Chair Factory in Riverton. Seth Thomas started his clockworks in Thomaston in 1812. Actor William Gillette built a castle in East Haddam with the money he made playing Sherlock Holmes at the turn of the century. In Mystic you can walk the decks of whaling ships and square-riggers, and in Groton tour the first nuclear-powered submarine, the U.S.S. *Nautilus*.

Where is the single best place in Connecticut? Well, a good place to research that question is Wesleyan University's library in Middletown. The original manuscript of Einstein's theory of relativity can be found there.

The Southeast

OAK ALLEY PLANTATION, VACHERIE, LOUISIANA

Fields of King Cotton, the sweet scent of magnolia blossoms, stately riverboats gently paddling by, catfish dinners, a guitar player singing the blues—it's surprising how many images most of us carry of Mississippi.

The stronghold of the Old South, Mississippi has changed a lot over the past few decades in some ways and hasn't changed at all in others. More than half the population still makes its living from the soil, though new jobs in industries like furniture, lumber, paper, food processing, and machinery have come to the state. Antebellum homes with names like Melrose, Shadowlawn, Dunleith, and Auburn still stand proudly in river towns, while black enrollment at Ole Miss climbs past the 7 percent mark.

Mississippi offers a rich diversity of scenery and traditions: historic towns like Vicksburg and Natchez; the beach resorts of Biloxi and the Gulf Coast; oil country in the northwest; Jackson, the state's only big city; the fabled Mississippi Delta region; the piney woods and crawling kudzu vines of the hill country around Oxford.

To keep its traditions alive, museums throughout the state commemorate everyone from Dizzy Dean to Casey Jones to the Choctaw Indians. None perhaps is more representative of the real Mississippi than the Biedenharn Candy Museum. It was here that Joseph Biedenharn had the southern ingenuity to bottle Coca-Cola™ for the first time—so it could be taken to the workers in the cotton fields. Above a display of Coke™ memorabilia dating back to 1894, a legend reads "Coca-Cola is a sublimated essence of all that America stands for—a decent thing honestly made."

Mississippi
THE MAGNOLIA STATE

THE DELTA QUEEN, MISSISSIPPI RIVER

57

ORIGIN OF NAME
From Indian words for the river, meaning "father of waters"

CAPITAL
Jackson

STATE FLOWER
Magnolia

STATE BIRD
Mockingbird

YEAR OF STATEHOOD
1817 (20th state)

FAMOUS MISSISSIPPIANS
Dana Andrews, William Faulkner, Leontyne Price, Charlie Pride, Eudora Welty, Oprah Winfrey, Richard Wright

THE MISSOURI MONUMENT,
VICKSBURG NATIONAL MILITARY PARK

BEAUVOIR, HOME OF JEFFERSON DAVIS, BILOXI

BALD CYPRESS SWAMP, NATCHEZ TRACE

JACKSON

STATE FAIR, JACKSON

FOLKLIFE FESTIVAL, DURHAM

North Carolina

THE TAR HEEL STATE

In 1587, supplies ran out at the small colony sponsored by Sir Walter Raleigh on North Carolina's Roanoke Island. England was at war, however, and could not send help until the Spanish Armada was defeated three years later. By then it was too late. The colony, including Virginia Dare, the first baby born to English parents in America, had vanished into thin air. Later, pirates roamed the coast's secret coves, and hundreds of ships were lost on the Diamond Shoals off Cape Hatteras, the "graveyard of the Atlantic."

Today, the state is less forbidding. In fact, gracious hospitality is North Carolina's hallmark. Thanks to cities like Greensboro, Winston-Salem, Charlotte, and Raleigh, it is also an important industrial center—the nation's largest producer of furniture, tobacco, brick, and textiles.

Flat coastal plains characterize one side of the state, including the famous golfing country of the Sandhills and, of course, Kitty Hawk, where the Wright Brothers made their historic flight over the dunes. Western North Carolina explodes into spectacular mountains—the Blue Ridge, Great Smoky, Black Craggy, Pisgah, and Balsam ranges all are here.

They used to say that the only way to get to Boone (founded by Daniel Boone) was to be born there, but these days the North Carolina mountains, with their rock climbing, rafting, skiing, and crafts, are open to all. You can even tour the magnificent 255-room Vanderbilt mansion, Biltmore, modeled after a 16th-century Loire Valley château.

And lest you think that North Carolina is just a place to turn off your brain and enjoy the scenery, the Research Triangle of Raleigh/Durham and Chapel Hill, with its three universities (Duke, North Carolina State, and the University of North Carolina) names more Ph.D.'s per capita than anywhere else in America.

PRICE LAKE, NEAR BLOWING ROCK

WHITEWATER RAFTING, THE NANTAHALA RIVER

CAPE HATTERAS LIGHTHOUSE

BURLEY TOBACCO FIELD,
WESTERN NORTH CAROLINA

WINSTON-SALEM

COUNTRY STORE, WATAUGA COUNTY

CHIMNEY ROCK PARK, CHIMNEY ROCK

STATE FAIR, RALEIGH

WRIGHT BROTHERS NATIONAL MEMORIAL,
KITTY HAWK

ORIGIN OF NAME
In honor of Charles I of England
("Carolus" is Latin for Charles)

CAPITAL
Raleigh

STATE FLOWER
Dogwood

STATE BIRD
Cardinal

YEAR OF STATEHOOD
1789 (12th state)

FAMOUS NORTH CAROLINIANS
Richard Gatling, Billy Graham,
O. Henry, Dolley Madison, Edward
R. Murrow, James K. Polk, Thomas
Wolfe

Kentucky
THE BLUEGRASS STATE

Imagine what this wild wondrous place must have looked like in 1769 to Daniel Boone, who blazed the Wilderness Trail through a natural gap in the rugged Appalachian Mountains, emerging on the hilly Cumberland Plateau—Kentucky! The "Great Meadow," he called it.

Today, Kentucky is still beautiful and inviting, a land of bluegrass hills and pastures, tobacco and coal, spectacular caves, independent people—and horses.

Each year the horse racing universe convenes in Louisville for the 10-day extravaganza called The Kentucky Derby Festival. The state has much more to offer than mint juleps and Churchill Downs, though you'd never know it on the first Saturday in May when they "Run for the Roses."

Broadway producers regularly travel to the renowned Actor's Theatre of Louisville in search of new plays, and the city produces everything from fine whiskey to world-famous baseball bats ("Louisville Sluggers"). Students from Appalachia at Berea College enjoy free tuition while keeping mountain crafts alive. Mammoth Cave in the western Pennyroyal (pronounced "Pennyrile") region is the world's largest cave system, and the state is home to historical attractions ranging from settlements of Shakers to Lincoln's birthplace.

How do natives really feel about their "Old Kentucky Home"? Well, in the booming city of Lexington, "Horse Capital of the World," is the Hunt Morgan House. During the Civil War, when Lexington was occupied by the North, Confederate Gen. John Hunt Morgan so longed for home that he sneaked through enemy lines into town. Pursued by Union troops, he rode his horse up the front stairs into the house, leaned down, kissed his mother, then charged out the back door.

THE KENTUCKY HORSE PARK, LEXINGTON

THE KENTUCKY CENTER FOR THE ARTS, LOUISVILLE

THE CUMBERLAND RIVER, PINEVILLE

LAND BETWEEN THE LAKES NATIONAL RECREATION AREA, WESTERN KENTUCKY

THE KENTUCKY DERBY, CHURCHILL DOWNS, LOUISVILLE

BELLE OF LOUISVILLE

66

HIGHLAND GAMES, GLASGOW

SHAKERTOWN AT PLEASANT HILL

THE DAVID APPALACHIAN CRAFT CO-OP, FLOYD COUNTY

ORIGIN OF NAME
Possibly from an Indian word
meaning "the land of tomorrow"

CAPITAL
Frankfort

STATE FLOWER
Goldenrod

STATE BIRD
Kentucky Cardinal

YEAR OF STATEHOOD
1792 (15th state)

FAMOUS KENTUCKIANS
Muhammad Ali, John James
Audubon, Daniel Boone, Louis D.
Brandeis, "Kit" Carson, Henry Clay,
Jefferson Davis, D. W. Griffith,
Robert Penn Warren

POLLY'S APPLE STAND, WESTMINSTER

DRAYTON HALL, CHARLESTON

MYRTLE BEACH

South Carolina
THE PALMETTO STATE

Life moves a little more slowly in South Carolina than in most places—at least some of the time.

The Deep South gentility of Charleston, for instance—an enchanting city of antebellum homes, hidden gardens, and winding cobblestone streets—makes you wonder how they ever could have named the dance after it.

Or take sleepy Georgetown, with its historic homes and memories of colonial rice and indigo plantations. It's hard to believe that the honky-tonk revelry of Myrtle Beach, where 12 million people vacation each summer, is only a few miles away.

In South Carolina, the modern luxury of Hilton Head Island, with its strict architectural code, shares the spotlight with Middleton Place, a historic plantation which has the oldest landscaped gardens in America, and Fort Sumter, where the opening shots of the Civil War were fired.

But let's return to Charleston, as all visitors long to. It's a place of old brick and fresh flowers, of culture and commerce, of moss-draped live oaks and she-crab soup. Charleston was the first city in the nation to establish a program to preserve its architectural heritage, and it shows—the skyline is still dominated by church steeples.

The Charleston Museum was the first museum in the United States. The Dock Street Theatre here was the first building in America designed for theatrical use. The oldest Baptist congregation and oldest Unitarian Church in the South are in Charleston. So is the oldest synagogue in continuous use in America.

How do Charlestonians view their city? "The place where the Ashley and Cooper rivers flow together to form the Atlantic Ocean," they say with either a straight face or a twinkle, depending upon how energetic they feel that day.

THE DOCK STREET THEATER, CHARLESTON

ORIGIN OF NAME
In honor of Charles I of England
("Carolus" is Latin for Charles)

CAPITAL
Columbia

STATE FLOWER
Yellow Jessamine

STATE BIRD
Carolina Wren

YEAR OF STATEHOOD
1788 (8th state)

FAMOUS SOUTH CAROLINIANS
John C. Calhoun, DuBose Heyward,
Ernest F. Hollings, Andrew Jackson,
Francis Marion, Thomas Sumter,
Strom Thurmond

HARBOR TOWN, HILTON HEAD ISLAND

THE CITADEL MILITARY COLLEGE, CHARLESTON

THE RIVERBANKS ZOO, COLUMBIA

FORT SUMTER NATIONAL MONUMENT, CHARLESTON

THE OGLETHORPE STATUE, SAVANNAH

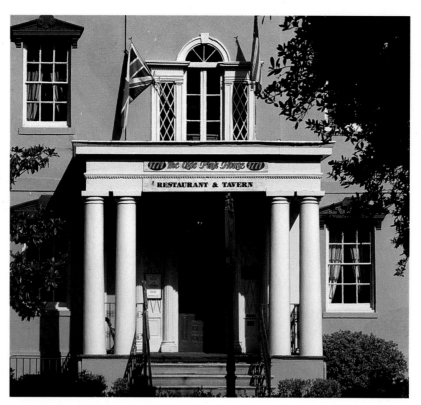

THE OLDE PINK HOUSE, SAVANNAH

QUILTING, HIAWASSEE MOUNTAIN FAIR

FRUIT STAND

STONE MOUNTAIN PARK, ATLANTA

Where did FDR and the pirate Blackbeard die? Where were Coca-Cola™ and the cotton gin invented? Where was the use of anesthetics pioneered for surgery and America's first state university chartered? Where can you find the largest freshwater swamp in the United States and the nation's tallest hotel, the largest exposed granite monolith and second busiest airport?

The answer to all of these questions is Georgia.

The capital of the "New South," Georgia leads the nation in many products, including paper and board, grows twice as many peanuts as any other state, and produces more than half of the world's pine resins and turpentine.

While Atlanta, communications and transportation center of the Southeast, has captured the world's admiration—470 of the Fortune 500 companies have offices here—Georgia is filled with other charming, historic places.

Savannah, the state's first settlement, is an achingly beautiful city of oaks hung with Spanish moss, swaying palmetto trees, and more than a thousand restored antebellum buildings—the nation's biggest urban historic district.

Augusta, once the world's largest inland cotton market, is now home of the world-famous Master's Golf Tournament, and adjacent Fort Gordon is the largest electronic communications training center in the world. The college town of Athens is aptly full of Greek Revival architecture and horticultural delights, while Georgia's subtropical "Golden Isles" near Brunswick, once havens for pirates, are now popular resorts. And everywhere are peach trees, red clay, and flowers.

One final question. What is the largest state east of the Mississippi? That's right, Georgia. No kidding.

Georgia

**THE PEACH STATE
EMPIRE STATE OF THE SOUTH**

THE HISTORIC DISTRICT, MADISON

ATLANTA

ORIGIN OF NAME
Named by founder James
Oglethorpe in honor of King
George II of England

CAPITAL
Atlanta

STATE FLOWER
Cherokee Rose

STATE BIRD
Brown Thrasher

YEAR OF STATEHOOD
1788 (4th state)

FAMOUS GEORGIANS
Jim Bowie, Erskine Caldwell, Jimmy
Carter, Ty Cobb, Martin Luther
King, Jr., Sidney Lanier, Margaret
Mitchell, Jackie Robinson

Virginia is for lovers. It is also for soldiers and statesmen, hikers and fishermen, architects and ship-builders, and half the office workers in Washington, D.C.

American history began and triumphed in Virginia.

Jamestown (remember John Smith and Pocahontas?) was the site of the first permanent English-speaking colony in the New World. Patrick Henry declared, "Give me liberty or give me death" in Richmond, not far from Yorktown, where British Gen. Lord Cornwallis surrendered in 1781, effectively ending the Revolutionary War.

George Washington and seven other presidents were born in Virginia. More than half the battles of the Civil War were fought here. And in Arlington National Cemetary—carved out of the estate of Robert E. Lee's wife—America's military heroes are buried.

Today, you can still taste history firsthand at Williamsburg, the colonial capital. It was lovingly restored beginning in 1926—America's first re-created community—and offers an authentic glimpse into 18th-century life.

You can also see some of the nation's most gorgeous scenery in the valley between the Blue Ridge and Allegheny Mountains. "Shenandoah," the Indians called it: Daughter of the Stars.

Virginia bursts with historic architecture ranging from the sublime—Mount Vernon, Monticello, and the University of Virginia (the latter two designed by Thomas Jefferson)—to the gargantuan. The Pentagon in Arlington is the world's largest office building with 17½ miles of corridors.

And lest you think Virginia is all hunt country and history, the East Coast Surfing Championships are held each year at Virginia Beach.

Virginia

THE OLD DOMINION

FARM NEAR CHARLOTTESVILLE

CHANCELLORSVILLE BATTLEFIELD

SHENANDOAH NATIONAL PARK

75

MONTICELLO, THOMAS JEFFERSON'S HOME, CHARLOTTESVILLE

ORIGIN OF NAME
In honor of Elizabeth I, England's
"Virgin Queen"

CAPITAL
Richmond

STATE FLOWER
American Dogwood

STATE BIRD
Cardinal

YEAR OF STATEHOOD
1788 (10th state)

FAMOUS VIRGINIANS
Patrick Henry, Thomas Jefferson,
Gen. Robert E. Lee, Meriwether
Lewis and William Clark, James
Madison, Edgar Allan Poe, George
Washington, Woodrow Wilson

YORKTOWN BATTLEFIELD

76

MOUNT VERNON, GEORGE WASHINGTON'S HOME

THE TOMB OF THE UNKNOWNS, ARLINGTON NATIONAL CEMETARY

COLONIAL WILLIAMSBURG

THE MONUMENT AVENUE FAIR, RICHMOND

MUSIC ROW, NASHVILLE

TENNESSEE WALKING HORSE FARM, CENTRAL TENNESSEE

Eastern Tennessee is magnificent hill country (the 800-square-mile Great Smoky Mountains National Park is the most visited national park in America). The state's central plains of rolling farmlands and bluegrass are dominated by the rhinestone glitter of Nashville. To the west is Memphis and the Mississippi River, which preserves a more traditionally "Southern" way of life.

But everywhere in Tennessee there's music. W. C. Handy was the first to put the blues down in written form on Beale Street in Memphis, not far from Graceland, home of Elvis Presley, the king of rock 'n' roll. Nashville is the country music capital of the world with several major record companies and the Grand Ole Opry.

More than a third of the population of Tennessee lives in three urban areas: Nashville, Memphis (named by one of its founders, Andrew Jackson, after the first capital of ancient Egypt), and beautiful Knoxville, resplendent with the pink and white blossoms of a million dogwood trees.

Lynchburg has the Jack Daniels Distillery. The 600-acre natural rhododendron garden atop Roan Mountain outside Elizabethton is said to be the world's largest. In Chattanooga there are scenic battlefields and historic railroads —the Chattanooga Choo Choo was the first passenger train to connect the North and South, and the Lookout Mountain Incline Railroad is the steepest in the world. Nashville and Memphis, however, still dominate the state's burgeoning tourist industry with their historic homes, gardens, and museums—and of course music.

One final note. Memphis, tired of being upstaged by Nashville (which calls itself the "Athens of the South" and boasts the world's only full-scale replica of the Parthenon), is now building—you guessed it—a pyramid.

Tennessee
THE VOLUNTEER STATE

WILD FLOWERS, CENTRAL TENNESSEE

THE PARTHENON, CENTENNIAL PARK, NASHVILLE

TOBACCO FIELD, EASTERN TENNESSEE

MEMPHIS IN MAY INTERNATIONAL FESTIVAL

ORIGIN OF NAME
"Tanasi" was the name of a
Cherokee settlement on the Little
Tennessee River

CAPITAL
Nashville

STATE FLOWER
Iris

STATE BIRD
Mockingbird

YEAR OF STATEHOOD
1796 (16th state)

FAMOUS TENNESSEANS
Davy Crockett, David Farragut,
Tennessee Ernie Ford, Grace Moore,
Patricia Neal, Dolly Parton, Elvis
Presley, Dinah Shore, Alvin York

STATUE OF ELVIS PRESLEY, MEMPHIS

THE GRAND OLE OPRY, NASHVILLE

TENNESSEE CRAFTS FAIR, NASHVILLE

THE JACK DANIELS DISTILLERY, NASHVILLE

Alabama

HEART OF DIXIE

The spot where Jefferson Davis took office as President of the Confederacy, the pulpit from which Martin Luther King launched the civil rights movement, the water pump where Helen Keller learned to speak her first word—all these can be found in Alabama, a place which recently has been billing itself as the "State of Surprises."

There are forests and hills in the north, bayous and rich black loam in the south, but it is the urban areas that have increasingly dominated the life of the state as it transforms its economic base from agriculture to industry.

Birmingham, Alabama's largest city, has revitalized its downtown and become one of the South's most progressive metropolitan areas. Montgomery has built a $21.5 million theater complex to house the renowned Alabama Shakespeare Festival. Huntsville has the state's largest district of antebellum architecture, yet is home to the Alabama Space and Rocket Center, the largest space museum in the world.

Alabama still has its moss-veiled live oaks, its banks of azaleas, and its gracious homes resplendent with white columns and wrought iron. And, though there's poverty, Alabama is still trying to pull itself up by its bootstraps. Alabamians have always tried to make the best of what they have.

After all, it was here at Tuskegee Institute (founded by Booker T. Washington, a former slave) that Dr. George Washington Carver showed that he could prepare a full meal with just one ingredient —the peanut.

And when boll weevils destroyed the cotton harvest in Enterprise shortly after the turn of the century, Alabamians built a monument to the pest—being forced to diversify their crops had brought on an economic boom!

STURDIVANT HALL, SELMA

DIE HARD 500, TALLADEGA

ORIGIN OF NAME
May come from an Indian tribe called the Alibamu, which means "I cleared the thicket"

CAPITAL
Montgomery

STATE FLOWER
Camellia

STATE BIRD
Yellowhammer

YEAR OF STATEHOOD
1819 (22nd state)

FAMOUS ALABAMIANS
Henry Aaron, Tallulah Bankhead, Hugo Black, George Washington Carver, Nat "King" Cole, Helen Keller, Joe Louis, Booker T. Washington, Hank Williams

THE GEORGE WASHINGTON CARVER MUSEUM, TUSKEGEE INSTITUTE, TUSKEGEE

District of Columbia

WASHINGTON IS A CAPITAL CITY

The District of Columbia is not a state, of course, but the nation's capital, Washington, the focal point of the American system of government. It is a great city with an illustrious history and more cultural attractions than many states. Its spirit is of the people, by the people, and for the people. Washington, D.C., is a reflection of us all.

George Washington appointed French engineer Pierre L'Enfant (who had come over with Lafayette) to plan the new nation's capital in 1791—the first city ever to be designed for a specific purpose: government. L'Enfant vowed it would rival the great capitals of Europe, with wide tree-lined avenues and bold plazas—and indeed Washington is unique among American cities in its majesty, order, and beauty.

Washington is divided into four quadrants, with the Capitol, where the Senate and House of Representatives meet, at its center. From the Capitol's steps, you can look out across the vast National Mall, past the Washington Monument, to the solemn Lincoln Memorial beyond.

Lining the Mall are several of the buildings of the world's largest museum complex—the Smithsonian Institution, America's national attic, where everything from space ships to African art to Archie Bunker's chair is displayed. Also on the Mall can be found one of the world's great art collections— the National Gallery—as well as the 58,156 names engraved into the V-shaped black granite walls of the Vietnam Veterans Memorial.

The Jefferson Memorial, the Library of Congress, the Kennedy Center for the Performing Arts ... there is much more in the nation's capital than can be described here. In fact, there is more than can even be seen in a week—though each year nearly 20 million visitors do their best. Happily, Washington has the fourth-largest concentration of hotel rooms of any city in the world (more than 43,000).

One family gets free lodging in a large white house on Pennsylvania Avenue. Their stay, however, is strictly dependent upon the pleasure of the people.

THE JEFFERSON MEMORIAL

THE VIETNAM VETERANS MEMORIAL

THE U.S. CAPITOL

GEORGETOWN

UNION STATION

PANDAS, NATIONAL ZOO

THE NATIONAL GALLERY OF ART

THE OLD POST OFFICE

LIBRARY OF CONGRESS

THE LINCOLN MEMORIAL

THE WHITE HOUSE

NATIONAL AIR & SPACE MUSEUM,
THE SMITHSONIAN INSTITUTION

THE WASHINGTON MONUMENT

West Virginia
THE MOUNTAIN STATE

When the Civil War broke out, Virginia split in two, the western regions choosing to remain with the Union. It was here in West Virginia, in fact, at lovely Harpers Ferry, where the Shenandoah meets the Potomac River and three states (Maryland, Virginia, and West Virginia) converge, that abolitionist John Brown seized the U.S. arsenal in his doomed attempt to free the slaves.

The state is still mostly wild, beautiful country, dominated by mountains—terrain so rugged that the Indians only hunted here, never settled. Forests cover more than 75 percent of the state, though West Virginia's mines produce one-fifth of the nation's coal.

Charleston, the state capital, is one of the nation's top glass and chemical producers. Berkeley Springs, the oldest spa in America, was popularized by George Washington, who frequently brought his whole family there. Nearby Charles Town, where John Brown was jailed and then hanged after his raid, was named for Washington's younger brother, Charles, who planned the city, naming its streets after relatives.

West Virginia is the home of the National Radio Astronomy Observatory; the New River Gorge Bridge, the world's longest single-arch steel span (the New River, ironically, is one of the oldest rivers in North America); the famous Greenbrier Resort in White Sulphur Springs, where America's first golf course was laid out; and Prabhupada's Palace of Gold, a 10-room, gold-domed Hindu shrine built by the Hare Krishnas on their commune, New Vrindaban.

And it was here, in Grafton, West Virginia, in 1907, that Anna Jarvis's mother died. Mrs. Jarvis celebrated the anniversary of the event to honor her mother and the idea caught on nationally. In 1914, President Woodrow Wilson made it official. We call it Mother's Day.

CANAAN VALLEY

HARPER'S FERRY

FERN CREEK FALLS, FAYETTE COUNTY

COAL MINE, PRENTER

ORIGIN OF NAME
From the western counties of Virginia that formed their own state in 1863 and the "Virgin Queen," Elizabeth I of England

CAPITAL
Charleston

STATE FLOWER
Big Rhododendron

STATE BIRD
Cardinal

YEAR OF STATEHOOD
1863 (35th state)

FAMOUS WEST VIRGINIANS
Newton D. Baker, Pearl S. Buck, Gen. Thomas J. "Stonewall" Jackson, Don Knotts, Cyrus Vance, Gen. Chuck Yeager

MIAMI BEACH

ART DECO DISTRICT, MIAMI BEACH

GASPARILLA, TAMPA

THE JOHN AND MABEL RINGLING MUSEUM OF ART, SARASOTA

Florida
THE SUNSHINE STATE

The oldest city in America or the "Experimental Prototype Community of Tomorrow"? Retirement haven for senior citizens or "Spring Break Capital of the World" for college kids? Subtropical wilderness or high-tech manufacturing center? Where do you begin describing Florida?

A state of contrasts, Florida hosts three times as many visitors as it has residents each year. They used to come for the white sands and sunshine of Miami Beach (right after World War II, Miami Beach built more hotels than the rest of the world combined), but these days the fun is everywhere.

Orlando is the world's premier vacation site thanks to Walt Disney World, Sea World, and the new Disney/MGM Studios and Universal Studios theme parks. Tampa, one of the fastest-growing cities in America, boasts Busch Gardens. Untold thousands flock to the Kennedy Space Center's Spaceport U.S.A. at Cape Canaveral, to the 1.4 million acres of the Everglades National Park, to the races at Hialeah.

But it's still the climate that makes it all work. From Jacksonville, the second largest city in the United States (in terms of square miles), to Palm Beach, where the rich and famous have played since the days of John D. Rockefeller; from Fort Myers, where many of Thomas A. Edison's original light bulbs still burn in his winter lab, to Little Havana in Miami, where some of the newest Americans make their homes, the weather in Florida is simply marvelous.

What else is there to do and see? Well, in and around Miami there's the Miccosukee Indian Village, Parrot Jungle, and the Orange Bowl. You can visit Tupperware World Headquarters in Orlando, as well as the Elvis Presley Museum. The spring that Ponce de León thought was the Fountain of Youth is in St. Augustine. There's Hemingway's house on Key Largo. St. Petersburg has the Salvador Dali Museum. . . . The list goes on and on.

THE MAGIC KINGDOM, WALT DISNEY WORLD

ORIGIN OF NAME
Florida means "full of flowers" in
Spanish, and Ponce de León, who
named the state, landed here on
Easter Sunday (*Pascua florida*) in
1513

CAPITAL
Tallahassee

STATE FLOWER
Orange Blossom

STATE BIRD
Mockingbird

YEAR OF STATEHOOD
1845 (27th state)

FAMOUS FLORIDIANS
Henry M. Flagler, MacKinlay Kantor,
Henry B. Plant, Marjorie Kinnan
Rawlings, Burt Reynolds, Joseph W.
Stilwell, Charles P. Summerall

THE DISNEY-MGM STUDIO THEME PARK, LAKE BUENA VISTA

THE JOHN F. KENNEDY SPACE CENTER

THE TAMPA BALLET

EVERGLADES NATIONAL PARK

FARM NEAR BURLINGTON, WISCONSIN

The Midwest

Michigan
THE WOLVERINE STATE

The two peninsulas of Michigan (connected by one of the world's longest suspension bridges) between them hold the busy hub of America's automobile industry as well as some of its least-touched wildernesses.

You're never more than 85 miles from one of the Great Lakes in Michigan. The state borders four of the five of them (Michigan, Superior, Erie, and Huron), giving it a shoreline longer than the distance from Florida to Maine. The 36,000 miles of streams, nearly 4 million acres of state forests, and 11,000 lakes make northern Michigan prime vacationland.

Detroit, of course, is the state's largest city—home of baseball's Tigers, Motown Records, and the automobile industry. Its downtown riverfront has undergone a glamorous redevelopment lately, offering real hope for the city's meaner streets.

Outside of Detroit in the suburb of Dearborn you can find the colossal Henry Ford Museum and Greenfield Village, 240 acres of historic buildings, including the Wright Brother's bicycle shop and the courtroom where Lincoln practiced law.

Lansing has big auto plants, Ann Arbor's famed Wolverines play in the country's largest college-owned football stadium (capacity 101,701), and Traverse City is the cherry capital of the world, producing 50 percent of the world's sweet and tart cherries.

From such enterprises as the Suicide Hill Ski Jumping Tournament in Ishpeming, the National Mushroom Hunting Championship in Boyne City, and the National Soaring and Hang Gliding Festivals in Frankfort and Elberta, it's clear that Michiganians like to have fun. Only, what do you suppose goes on at the Carry Nation Festival in Holly?

FLINT BALLOON FESTIVAL AND AIR RACE, GENESSEE COUNTY

THE SPARTANS, MICHIGAN STATE UNIVERSITY, EAST LANSING

PLYMOUTH ICE SCULPTURE SPECTACULAR, PLYMOUTH

THE RENAISSANCE CENTER, DETROIT

TULIP TIME FESTIVAL, HOLLAND

CRANBROOK INSTITUTE OF ARTS AND SCIENCES, BLOOMFIELD HILLS

THE GENERAL MOTORS BUILDING, DETROIT

ORIGIN OF NAME
From Chippewa words "mici" and "gama," meaning "great water"

CAPITAL
Lansing

STATE FLOWER
Apple Blossom

STATE BIRD
Robin

YEAR OF STATEHOOD
1837 (26th state)

FAMOUS MICHIGANIANS
Ralph Bunche, Edna Ferber, Gerald R. Ford, Henry Ford, Aretha Franklin, Lee Iacocca, Magic Johnson, Joe Louis, Madonna, Diana Ross, Tom Selleck

Indiana

THE HOOSIER STATE

People don't think of Indians any more when they think of Indiana, but the state was named for its original inhabitants, who battled ferociously for their territories. Pontiac ended his rebellion in 1766 by literally burying his hatchet, but uprisings continued until William Henry Harrison's troops defeated Tecumseh's brother, the Prophet, at Tippecanoe in 1811.

Nowadays, Indiana is a place of cornfields and quaint round barns, white sand beaches on Lake Michigan, gentle hills, and charming river towns, the bustling industry of the north—and sports!

Every Memorial Day thousands of racing fans make a pilgrimage to Indianapolis to witness the Superbowl of car racing, the Indy 500. Indiana is a state where basketball is practically a religion, where Notre Dame's Fighting Irish are as popular as rock stars, and where they even make movies about bicycle races (*Breaking Away*).

Indiana is unique among her Midwest neighbors in many ways. The state is host to the Beanblossom Music Festival, one of the nation's largest bluegrass events. Parke County claims to have more covered bridges than any other county in the United States. Robert Indiana's famous *LOVE* sculpture is here. So is the John Dillinger Historical Museum.

Why do they call themselves "Hoosiers"? One theory goes back to a contractor named Samuel Hoosier who built the Ohio Falls Canal in 1826. Mr. Hoosier preferred to hire laborers from the Indiana side of the river, so his work gang came to be called Hoosier's. Another theory, which points to the long Indiana tradition of friendliness and hospitality, holds that "Hoosier" is just a contraction of the early pioneers' way of answering the door, "Who's here?"

UNION STATION, INDIANAPOLIS

THE HOOSIERS, INDIANA UNIVERSITY, BLOOMINGTON

THE INDIANAPOLIS ZOO

ORIGIN OF NAME
Means "land of the Indians"

CAPITAL
Indianapolis

STATE FLOWER
Peony

STATE BIRD
Cardinal

YEAR OF STATEHOOD
1816 (19th state)

FAMOUS "HOOSIERS"
Larry Bird, Hoagy Carmichael, James Dean, Theodore Dreiser, Gil Hodges, Cole Porter, Red Skelton

THE INDY 500, INDIANAPOLIS MOTOR SPEEDWAY

GUADALUPE MOUNTAINS NATIONAL PARK

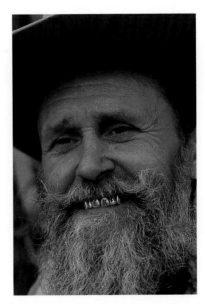

RANCH ROUNDUP, WICHITA FALLS

Texas

THE LONE STAR STATE

Texas is bigger than France, more populous than Australia, and so diverse that within its borders you can find everything from citrus groves to deserts, jagged mountains to marshland.

Oil money built Houston, America's fourth-largest city, and with its hot humid climate, the most air-conditioned place in the world. Home of the Astrodome and Johnson Space Center, its glittering skyline has few buildings more than 25 years old.

Executives in cowboy boots and Stetsons really do walk the streets of Dallas, a slick, sophisticated town full of new hotels and friendly people. Her sister city, Fort Worth, is an old-fashioned cow town that boasts three superb museums: the Kimbell, for ancient art and old master paintings; the Amon Carter, with its Remingtons and Russells; and a contemporary collection at the Modern Art Museum.

Hip, centrally-located Austin is the state capital and home to the Texas-sized University of Texas (enrollment is more than 75,000), the wealthiest public university in America. A Gutenberg Bible is on display in its library, and one of its dorms is big enough to have its own zip code.

Over 1.2 million people live in San Antonio, where five historic missions and the most visited shrine in Texas, the Alamo, can be found.

From the palm-lined beaches of Corpus Christi to the wildlife and scenic canyons of Big Bend National Park, from the high plains of Amarillo and Lubbock to the fertile Rio Grande Valley, Texas has just about everything.

And under the terms of its 1845 annexation agreement, Texas can subdivide into as many as five states any time it wants to, which would give Texans the extra political clout of eight more senators, four more governors, and several additional votes in the Electoral College!

HOUSTON

PRESIDIO LA BAHIA, GOLIAD

DALLAS

THE DALLAS BALLET

OUTH PADRE ISLAND, GULF COAST

THE ALAMO, SAN ANTONIO

MAYAN DUDE RANCH, BANDERA

MISSION CONTROL, THE LYNDON B. JOHNSON SPACE CENTER, CLEAR LAKE

BIG BEND NATIONAL PARK

SIX FLAGS OVER TEXAS, ARLINGTON

THE DALLAS MUSEUM OF ART

PASEO DEL RIO AT CHRISTMAS, SAN ANTONIO

THE HOUSTON ASTRODOME

ORIGIN OF NAME
From a Caddo Indian word meaning "friends"

CAPITAL
Austin

STATE FLOWER
Bluebonnet

STATE BIRD
Mockingbird

YEAR OF STATEHOOD
1845 (28th state)

FAMOUS TEXANS
Stephen F. Austin, Carol Burnett, Dwight D. Eisenhower, Sam Houston, Howard Hughes, Lyndon Johnson, Mary Martin, Chester Nimitz, Katharine Ann Porter

This is the land of amber waves of grain. Kansas produces more wheat than any other state (or even most nations). Looking over the lush farms and green empty pastureland, it's hard to believe that the state could have had such a violent history.

"Bleeding Kansas" they called this region in pre-Civil War days, so fierce was the fighting between pro- and antislavery factions. After the war, thousands of longhorn steers were driven through the state, making Dodge City, a cow town stopover on the Sante Fe Trail, into the "Wickedest Little City in America." So many gunslingers died with their boots on that the impromptu cemetery was nicknamed Boot Hill. At one point the town had a saloon for every 50 citizens, among them Wyatt Earp, Bat Masterson, and "Doc" Holliday.

In this century, locusts, dust storms, and droughts have plagued the state; but every Kansas farmer is still productive enough to feed himself and 75 others.

Besides being America's bread basket, Kansas is an important transportation, milling, and mining center, and home to the Menninger Clinic and Foundation, a famed research, teaching, and treatment center for mental illness. Kansas is also the nation's leading helium producer and the "Air Capital of the World." Beech, Boeing, Cessna, and Lear all manufacture aircraft in Wichita, the state's largest city.

What is Kansas's most surprising attraction? The Kansas Tourist Board votes for the Cosmosphere and Space Center in Hutchinson, but some think a better candidate can be found in the Museum of Natural History at the University of Kansas, Lawrence campus: the stuffed body of the only survivor of Custer's Last Stand—a horse named Comanche.

ORIGIN OF NAME
From the Sioux Indian word meaning "people of the south wind"

CAPITAL
Topeka

STATE FLOWER
Native Sunflower

STATE BIRD
Western Meadowlark

YEAR OF STATEHOOD
1861 (34th state)

FAMOUS KANSANS
Thomas Hart Benton, John Brown, Amelia Earhart, Dwight D. Eisenhower, "Wild Bill" Hickok, William Inge, Gordon Parks

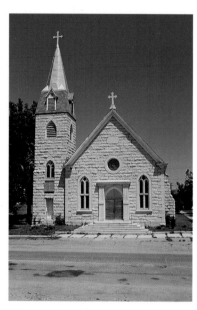

ST. ANTHONY'S CHURCH, STRONG CITY

WHEAT HARVEST, CENTRAL KANSAS

KANSAS STEER, CENTRAL KANSAS

GUNFIGHT REENACTMENT, DODGE CITY

Kansas

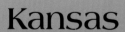

**THE JAYHAWK STATE
THE SUNFLOWER STATE**

REZAC LIVESTOCK AUCTION, ST. MARY'S

Illinois

THE PRAIRIE STATE

Rising on the shores of Lake Michigan, where the Great Plains meet the Great Lakes, Chicago is the industrial crown of Illinois, the transportation hub of the Midwest, and the pulsating center of the nation.

More than 8 million people, speaking 54 different languages and dialects, live in this metropolis that native poet Carl Sandburg called "City of the Big Shoulders." Steel, meatpacking, and politics are still some of Chicago's most famous products, but now finance, electronics, and publishing have become increasingly important. The world's tallest building, the world's busiest airport, the world's premier commodities market, and what is arguably the world's finest symphony orchestra all can be found here.

But Illinois is more than just one city.

Most of the state is rich farmland, a significant dairying center that leads the nation in agricultural exports. Though industrial, manufacturing, and mining activities are important throughout the state, there is still room for 4 million acres of woodlands in the southern Shawnee National Forest.

This is a land of corn and soybeans, of river towns, of restored Victorian villages, and Indian burial mounds. This is the Land of Lincoln—Springfield, Decatur, Charlestown, and New Salem all burst with mementos and memories of Illinois' martyred son, the 16th President of the United States.

And shrewd, sophisticated Chicago notwithstanding, heartland Illinois is where city slickers have always had to journey to find out "if it will play in Peoria."

CHICAGO

LINCOLN'S NEW SALEM STATE PARK, PETERSBURG

MERCHANDISE MART, CHICAGO

CHICAGO

CORNFIELD, CENTRAL ILLINOIS

LINCOLN'S NEW SALEM STATE PARK,
PETERSBURG

THE MISSISSIPPI RIVER

THE WORLD PORK EXPO, SPRINGFIELD

MICHIGAN AVENUE, CHICAGO

BUCKINGHAM FOUNTAIN, CHICAGO

THE LINCOLN HOME NATIONAL HISTORIC SITE, SPRINGFIELD

THE ART INSTITUTE OF CHICAGO

ORIGIN OF NAME
From adding a French suffix to an Indian word meaning "tribe of superior men"

CAPITAL
Springfield

STATE FLOWER
Native Violet

STATE BIRD
Cardinal

YEAR OF STATEHOOD
1818 (21st state)

FAMOUS ILLINOISANS
Saul Bellow, Jack Benny, Ray Bradbury, Clarence Darrow, Ulysses S. Grant, Ernest Hemingway, Abraham Lincoln, Ronald Reagan, Frank Lloyd Wright

Nebraska
THE CORNHUSKER STATE

Vast grasslands, ranches, and verdant farms cover 93 percent of Nebraska, a state that with the Oregon Trail, the Mormon Trail, and the Lewis and Clark Trail, was practically a superhighway for the American pioneers.

Some 350,000 traders, settlers, and missionaries passed through the state from 1840 to 1866, some choosing to stay and make their homes on the plains. Ironically, what an 1819 explorer called the "Great American Desert . . . almost wholly unfit for cultivation," has become a breadbasket for the world.

Cultivating more varieties of grass than any other state, and with bumper crops of wheat, rye, and corn, Nebraska is a leading agricultural producer. The state's huge cattle and hog industries make Omaha and its surrounding area one of the nation's largest meat-packing centers.

Nebraska has larger underground water resources than any other inland state—estimated at nearly 1.9 billion acre-feet, enough water to cover the state to a depth of 34 feet. Still, the 20,000 square miles of Sandhills in the north-central portion of the state form a barren jewel, a treeless land of scrub brush and blowing tumbleweeds where cattle range and the mystique of the cowboy lives.

Nebraska is the state where Crazy Horse died, where Father Flanagan founded Boys Town, where the world's largest elephant fossil was found, and where the Strategic Air Command makes its headquarters (Omaha has the dubious honor of being on the Soviet Union's list of top five targets). It's the home of the National Museum of Roller Skating, the world's largest American Legion post . . . and some of the nicest people in the world.

CHIMNEY ROCK NATIONAL HISTORIC SITE, NEAR SCOTTS BLUFF

THE CENTRAL PARK MALL, OMAHA

ORIGIN OF NAME
An Otoe Indian word for the state's principal river, meaning "shallow water"

CAPITAL
Lincoln

STATE FLOWER
Goldenrod

STATE BIRD
Western Meadowlark

YEAR OF STATEHOOD
1867 (37th state)

FAMOUS NEBRASKANS
Fred Astaire, Marlon Brando, Dick Cavett, Johnny Carson, Willa Cather, Henry Fonda, Malcolm X

BUFFALO STEW COOKOUT, FT. ROBINSON, CRAWFORD

THE BUFFALO BILL RANCH, NORTH PLATTE

BOYS TOWN, OMAHA

THE CORNHUSKERS, UNIVERSITY OF NEBRASKA, LINCOLN

Arkansas
LAND OF OPPORTUNITY

In 1975, a tourist digging at the Crater of Diamonds State Park outside of Murfreesboro—the only active diamond mine in America—unearthed the 16.37-carat "Amarillo Starlight," proving conclusively that Arkansas is indeed the "land of opportunity." It's also a land of beautiful mountain scenery, vintage architecture, folk arts, and spa towns.

Little Rock, on the bank of the Arkansas River, is the state's capital and largest city, offering impressive historic districts and homes. The state legislature even meets in a scaled-down replica of the Capitol in Washington, D.C.

Hernando de Soto discovered the Hot Springs area in 1541, a valley of 47 thermal springs where everyone from Franklin D. Roosevelt to Al Capone has come to "take the waters." A million gallons flow out of the ground at 143 degrees Fahrenheit each day, water so pure that NASA used it to protect moon rocks from bacteria.

In the northern Ozarks, outside of the charming Victorian town of Eureka Springs, the hills are alive with the sound of banjo pickers and old-time fiddling. The Ozarks are some of the world's oldest mountains, but traditional crafts such as pottery, basketmaking, quilting, and wood carving are as fresh and vital here as ever.

Davy Crockett summed up what Arkansas is all about when he wrote in 1835, "There are some first-rate men there, of the half-horse, half-alligator breed, with a sprinkling of the steamboat, and such as grow nowhere on the face of the universal earth, but just about the backbone of North America."

WHITTAKER'S POINT, OZARK NATIONAL FOREST

MT. MAGAZINE FRONTIER DAYS, PARIS

SCARECROW, PONCA

ORIGIN OF NAME
A French variant for the Quapaw Sioux, the "downstream people"

CAPITAL
Little Rock

STATE FLOWER
Apple Blossom

STATE BIRD
Mockingbird

YEAR OF STATEHOOD
1836 (25th state)

FAMOUS ARKANSANS
Hattie Caraway, "Dizzy" Dean, Orval Faubus, James W. Fulbright, John L. McClellan, Winthrop Rockefeller, Edward Durell Stone

LITTLE ROCK

"America's Dairyland," proclaims Wisconsin's license plates, and it's no idle boast. Wisconsin produces nearly a fifth of the nation's milk, leading all the states in dairy production and the number of milk cows.

Other important Wisconsin products include machinery, paper, agriculture, and social legislation —the state pioneered pensions for the blind, aid to dependent children, old-age assistance, and unemployment compensation.

Milwaukee, on the shores of Lake Michigan, is Wisconsin's largest city, but with its large and diverse ethnic communities it feels more like a collection of small towns; there's a different festival or street party practically every weekend during the summer.

The influence of the German beer-making immigrants is still strong in Milwaukee, home of the Pabst Theater and the Schlitz Audubon Center. Even the city's pro baseball team is called the Brewers ("Bernie Brewer" chutes out of his chalet on the center field scoreboard into a gigantic mug of suds every time a Brewer hits a home run).

Wisconsin is full of notable places. Madison, the state capital, is home to the main campus of the huge University of Wisconsin. Green Bay has its renowned Packers football team. Even little Hayward holds the largest cross-country ski race in America each year.

Still, Door County, a 40-mile peninsula stretching north into Lake Michigan, is *the* place in America to go for fishboils, an old Scandinavian tradition. Basically, you just boil up a cauldron of whitefish, dump in a container of kerosene, and light it. Just be sure to stand back as the flames roar some 12 feet into the air.

Wisconsin
THE BADGER STATE

OLD WORLD THIRD STREET, MILWAUKEE

VILLA LOUIS, PRARIE DU CHIEN

124

FARM, NEAR BOYD

OLD WADE HOUSE, GREENBUSH

GREEN BAY PACKER HALL OF FAME

ORIGIN OF NAME
A Chippewa word believed to mean
"grassy place"

CAPITAL
Madison

STATE FLOWER
Wood Violet

STATE BIRD
Robin

YEAR OF STATEHOOD
1848 (30th state)

FAMOUS WISCONSINITES
Harry Houdini, Robert La Follette,
Alfred Lunt, Spencer Tracy, Orson
Welles, Thornton Wilder, Frank
Lloyd Wright

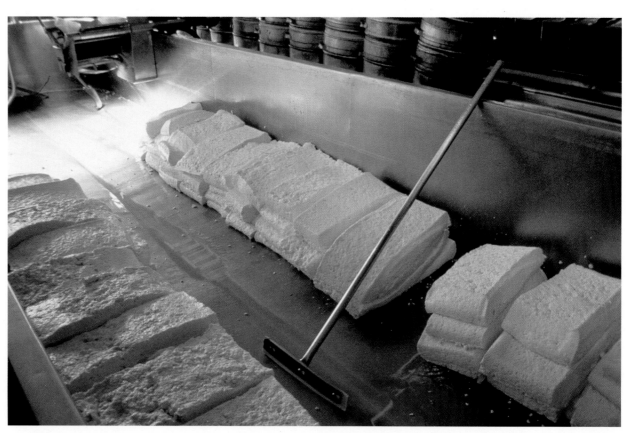

CHEESE FACTORY, FERRYVILLE

MITCHELL PARK HORTICULTURAL CONSERVATORY

U.S. INTERNATIONAL SNOW SCULPTING COMPETITION,
PERFORMING ARTS CENTER, MILWAUKEE

HENRY MEIER FESTIVAL PARK, MILWAUKEE

THE CORN PALACE, MITCHELL

THE BADLANDS NATIONAL MONUMENT, NEAR WALL

INDIAN GRAVEYARD,
WOUNDED KNEE BATTLEFIELD

In 1927, a 56-year-old sculptor named Gutzon Borglum, the son of Danish immigrants and a student of Auguste Rodin, began carving the likenesses of George Washington, Thomas Jefferson, Abraham Lincoln, and Theodore Roosevelt into the granite face of Mount Rushmore—granite so hard it is not expected to weather more than one inch every 5000 years.

When the memorial was completed shortly after Borglum's death 14 years later, it had cost only $1 million—a bargain considering that more than 2 million people visit Mount Rushmore each year.

Besides Mount Rushmore, South Dakota, a state of "savage extremes" in both temperature and terrain, boasts broad prairies, desolate Badlands, rich farms (the state ranks first in U.S. production of oats and rye), and the highest mountains east of the Rockies—the magnificent Black Hills.

The Treaty of 1868 gave the Black Hills and all of the state west of the Mississippi to the Sioux Indians. Just six years later, however, an expedition headed by none other than George Armstrong Custer discovered gold in the Black Hills. The treaty was forgotten in the ensuing gold rush, and Colonel Custer and his men suffered the consequences. Today, South Dakota is still first in U.S. gold production, with the largest operating mine in the Western Hemisphere.

Other South Dakota assets include spectacular parks, wildlife, and caves. The Black Hills National Forest alone covers nearly 1.25 million acres, and Jewel Cave is the fourth-longest cave in the world.

Finally, at Mount Moriah Cemetery in the quintessential Wild West town of Deadwood, can be found the remains of "Wild Bill" Hickok—shot dead in a poker game, holding aces and eights. Bill's friend "Calamity Jane" is buried at his side.

ORIGIN OF NAME
"Dakota" is Sioux for "friend" or "ally"

CAPITAL
Pierre

STATE FLOWER
American Pasqueflower

STATE BIRD
Ring-necked Pheasant

YEAR OF STATEHOOD
1889 (40th state)

FAMOUS SOUTH DAKOTANS
Tom Brokaw, Crazy Horse, Mary Hart, Cheryl Ladd, George McGovern, Billy Mills, Al Neuharth, Pat O'Brien

South Dakota

**THE COYOTE STATE
THE SUNSHINE STATE**

The land of Hiawatha and Paul Bunyan was carved out thousands of years ago by the retreat of mile-high glaciers, leaving Minnesota with more than 12,000 lakes— more shoreline than California, Hawaii, and Oregon combined. Nowadays, forests cover one-third of the land, and rivers full of walleye, northern pike, and other varieties crisscross the state (Minnesota offers more kinds of fishing than anywhere in America).

What else is Minnesota besides a natural wonderland? A major trade center, for one thing. Thanks to the St. Lawrence Seaway, Duluth has become the largest inland port in the world. The state is also a vital mining region—a few square miles in the state's northern mountain ranges produce more than 60 percent of the nation's iron ore. Corporate giants like 3M, General Mills, Pillsbury, and Honeywell make their headquarters here, as do more than 2000 high-tech companies.

It's a state where 91 percent of students graduate high school (best rate in the United States), where the world's largest unsupported marble dome can be found (the Minnesota state capitol), and where places like Garrison Keillor's "Lake Wobegon" still exist.

Most surprising, however, Minnesota is a great cultural center. Minneapolis and St. Paul (which used to be called Pig's Eye, after a one-eyed whiskey bootlegger) have scores of galleries, museums, and dance companies. The beautiful new Ordway Music Theatre is the home of America's first full-time chamber orchestra, and only New York City spends more on the performing arts or has more theaters per capita.

But then what would you expect from a state that could bring the world such disparate performers as Judy Garland, Bob Dylan, and Prince?

Minnesota

THE NORTH STAR STATE
THE GOPHER STATE

STRAWBERRY STAND, BLOOMINGTON

NORTHEASTERN MINNESOTA

THE METRODOME, MINNEAPOLIS

ANNUAL POWWOW, GRAND PORTAGE

131

INDEPENDENCE DAY PARADE, DELANO

ORIGIN OF NAME
From a Dakota Sioux Indian word meaning "land of sky-tinted water"

CAPITAL
St. Paul

STATE FLOWER
Showy (Pink and White) Lady's-slipper

STATE BIRD
Common Loon

YEAR OF STATEHOOD
1858 (32nd state)

FAMOUS MINNESOTANS
F. Scott Fitzgerald, Hubert Humphrey, Sinclair Lewis, Charles Lindbergh, E. G. Marshall, the Mayo brothers, Charles Schulz, Thorstein Veblen

THE GUTHRIE THEATER, MINNEAPOLIS

THE IDS BUILDING (LEFT) AND THE NORWEST TOWER, MINNEAPOLIS

MINNESOTA ZOOLOGICAL GARDEN, APPLE VALLEY

THE FOREST HISTORIC CENTER, GRAND RAPIDS

THE CHARLES A. LINDBERGH STATUE, ST. PAUL

THE KANSAS CITY ROYALS

THE MARK TWAIN MEMORIAL, HANNIBAL

The Gateway Arch, symbol of the spirit that opened the West, soars 630 feet above the Mississippi River at St. Louis. It's a starkly modern monument, breathtaking both in scale and simplicity, the tallest monument in the world, an architectural dream. But dreams are not enough for Missourians. They need to be shown.

Missouri is a place that has always specialized in hammering dreams into practical realities. The Pony Express was born here. So were the hot dog, the ice cream cone, and Budweiser beer. This is where Laura Ingalls Wilder wrote her "Little House" books, where Scott Joplin perfected ragtime, where Mark Twain turned a few boys on a raft into giants.

It's a state of great natural beauty. Sweeping plains in the east and north give way to lush mountains in the south. There are more known caves (5000) in Missouri than anywhere else in America, and parks, forests, lakes, and natural springs abound.

Both St. Louis and lively Kansas City (which claims to have more fountains and boulevards than Rome and Paris) have world-class orchestras and museums (St. Louis's was the first municipally supported art museum in America), but culture in Missouri is not confined to urban areas. A native hill culture with its traditional crafts still thrives in the Ozarks, and Branson near the Arkansas border rivals Nashville as a center for country music.

Missouri may demand to be shown, but in terms of culture, natural beauty, and realized dreams, it has a lot to show for itself.

Missouri

THE SHOW ME STATE

OLD SETTLER'S DAY, KOHOKA

COUNTRY CLUB PLAZA, KANSAS CITY

THE ST. LOUIS ART MUSEUM

TROUT FISHING, ROARING RIVER STATE PARK

ST. LOUIS

THE HARRY S TRUMAN NATIONAL HISTORIC SITE, INDEPENDENCE

ORIGIN OF NAME
From the Missouri (meaning "town of the large canoes") Indians

CAPITAL
Jefferson City

STATE FLOWER
Hawthorn

STATE BIRD
Bluebird

YEAR OF STATEHOOD
1821 (24th state)

FAMOUS MISSOURIANS
George Washington Carver, Walt Disney, T. S. Eliot, Jesse James, Gen. John J. Pershing, Harry S Truman, Mark Twain, Tennessee Williams

Iowa

THE HAWKEYE STATE

A state of lush, rolling countryside, Iowa produces 10 percent of America's food supply, leading the nation in all livestock marketing. The state's manufactured goods, however, are worth three times more than its agriculture, and enough insurance companies are headquartered in Des Moines to make it the third-largest insurance center in the world. Clearly, Iowans know how to work hard and work smart.

Of course, there's a lot more to Iowa than produce and productivity. There's greyhound racing in Dubuque, paddle boat rides down the Mississippi at Davenport, even skiing north of Council Bluffs. The state is full of historic Victorian houses, covered bridges, parks teeming with fish and game—and a heaping portion of good wholesome fun.

The National Balloon Museum in Indianola hosts a summertime hot air balloon competition. At Boone is the Kate Shelly High Bridge, the longest and highest double-track railroad bridge in the world. There's an authentic 1848 windmill in Elk Horn, the largest Danish settlement in the United States. Museums, woolen mills, and family restaurants characterize the Amana Colonies, where a German religious sect found refuge in 1855. And *People* magazine says that the best blueberry ice cream in America can be found in Iowa City.

In *The Music Man*, Meredith Willson painted Iowans at the turn of the century as stubborn, chip-on-the-shoulder folks who would give you the shirts off their backs if you ran into trouble.

These days, Iowans are still as independent and opinionated as ever. The *Des Moines Register*'s annual Iowa Poll reports that one out of every nine Iowans names his or her car, and while only 5 percent of the population expects to go to hell, 31 percent knows someone else who might end up there.

IOWA STATE FAIR, DES MOINES

THE HAWKEYES, UNIVERSITY OF IOWA, IOWA CITY

ORIGIN OF NAME
From an Indian word meaning the "Beautiful Land"

CAPITAL
Des Moines

STATE FLOWER
Wild Rose

STATE BIRD
Eastern Goldfinch

YEAR OF STATEHOOD
1846 (29th state)

FAMOUS IOWANS
"Buffalo Bill" Cody, Mamie Eisenhower, Herbert H. Hoover, Glenn Miller, John Wayne, Grant Wood

TOWN CLOCK AND COUNTY COURTHOUSE, DUBUQUE

FARM NEAR DES MOINES

North Dakota

THE SIOUX STATE
THE PEACE GARDEN STATE

When Teddy Roosevelt's wife and mother both died on the same day, he came to North Dakota's Badlands in search of "physical and spiritual renewal." Here, in the fantastic, almost lunar landscapes created by the meandering Little Missouri River, where wild horses, bighorn sheep, bison, deer, and antelope still roam, he found the strength to go on and eventually attain the presidency.

North Dakota today is the most rural of states. Only Kansas produces more wheat. Farms cover 90 percent of the land, which is mostly gentle and fertile plain, though Lake Sakakawea, with its 1600 miles of shoreline, bisects the western half of the state, and the north is dotted with lakes and wildlife refuges. A big city, by North Dakota standards, means Fargo with 61,000 people or Grand Forks with 44,000. The 18-story state capitol building in Bismarck (population 45,000) is considered a skyscraper.

Whether it's the wide open spaces or the manageable scale of things, people are genuinely friendly in North Dakota. It's not surprising, therefore, that on July 14, 1932, a crowd of 50,000 gathered not far from the geographic center of North America in Rugby to dedicate the International Peace Garden, celebrating Canadian-American friendship.

The dedication plaque of this beautiful and symbolic 2300-acre botanical monument to the world's longest undefended border speaks eloquently of the spirit of North Dakota: "We two nations dedicate this garden and pledge ourselves that as long as men shall live we will not take arms against one another."

BURKE COUNTY

GENE'S CAFE, BOWMAN

HARVESTING CORN, GRANT COUNTY

141

ORIGIN OF NAME
"Dakota" is Sioux for "friend" or "ally"

CAPITAL
Bismarck

STATE FLOWER
Wild Prairie Rose

STATE BIRD
Western Meadowlark

YEAR OF STATEHOOD
1889 (39th state)

FAMOUS NORTH DAKOTANS
Maxwell Anderson, Angie Dickinson, Louis L'Amour, Peggy Lee, Eric Sevareid, Lawrence Welk

COUPLE WITH HOMEMADE PHOTO STATUETTES, RUGBY

142

UNITED MINE WORKERS OF AMERICA
RALLY, BEULAH

HORSE RANCH, EMMONS COUNTY

SISTERS OF ST. FRANCIS CONVENT AND SCHOOL, HANKINSON

FT. UNION

LOUISIANA BAYOU

BOURBON STREET, NEW ORLEANS

LOUISIANA STATE UNIVERSITY, BATON ROUGE

Louisiana

THE PELICAN STATE

There's more to Louisiana than New Orleans.

The 34-story state capitol that Huey Long built in Baton Rouge, for instance, is the tallest in the nation. Natchilotches, the oldest permanent settlement in the Louisiana Purchase, has the fine Bayou Folk Museum and many historic structures. St. Martinsville is home of the Evangeline Oak, a meeting place made famous in Longfellow's poem. And everywhere is Louisiana's Cajun culture—named for the Acadian people, originally French settlers who were expelled from their homes in Nova Scotia by the English government in 1755 and resettled here.

But New Orleans (local folks call it "N'awlins") is the place where all the state's diverse elements—Cajun, French Creole, Spanish, African, and Native American—come together in a cultural jambalaya that is one of America's liveliest cities.

The "Big Easy" has a thousand different faces—the Dixieland joints on Bourbon Street; the tavern where Andrew Jackson met pirate Jean Lafitte; the oldest active Roman Catholic Cathedral in the U.S.; the Superdome, the world's largest enclosed stadium-arena; and, of course, Mardi Gras, when *Le Vieux Carré* is like no other place on earth.

Good food is practically a religion here. From your morning chicory *café au lait* and a *beignet* (a unique square doughnut with no hole), to an oyster po' boy and some praline candy for lunch, to a supper of gumbo or a crawfish *étouffée*, the city is a gastronomical delight.

It's no accident that the collision of ethnic influences in New Orleans first produced that uniquely American phenomenon, jazz. What is jazz? "Man, if you gotta ask," answered Louis Armstrong, "you'll never know."

145

THE GARDEN DISTRICT, NEW ORLEANS

JACKSON SQUARE, NEW ORLEANS

PRESERVATION HALL, NEW ORLEANS

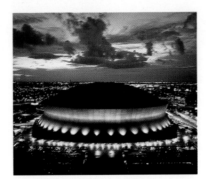

THE SUPERDOME, NEW ORLEANS

ST. JOHN'S CATHEDRAL, LAFAYETTE

MARDI GRAS, NEW ORLEANS

ORIGIN OF NAME
Named after an early owner—
French King Louis XIV

CAPITAL
Baton Rouge

STATE FLOWER
Magnolia Grandiflora

STATE BIRD
Eastern Brown Pelican

YEAR OF STATEHOOD
1812 (18th state)

FAMOUS LOUISIANANS
Louis Armstrong, Pierre Beauregard,
Judah P. Benjamin, Braxton Bragg,
Grace King, Huey Long, Henry
Miller Shreve, Edward D. White, Jr.

STATE FAIR, OKLAHOMA CITY

QUARTZ MOUNTAIN STATE PARK, NEAR ALTUS

"The corn is as high as a cow pony's eye," wrote Oscar Hammerstein II of this state in his and Richard Rodgers' ground-breaking musical, *Away We Go*. By the time the show opened, of course, that cow pony's eye had become an elephant's, and the musical had been renamed, *Oklahoma!*

At noon on April 22, 1889, a shot was fired and thousands of settlers eager to claim free homesteads swarmed over the borders and into the state we know as Oklahoma (it's nicknamed for those who beat the gun and got there *sooner*). By nightfall, Oklahoma City, which a few hours earlier had been an empty prairie, had 10,000 residents.

Today's Oklahoma, a land of high mesas, clear lakes, and wide open spaces, is built on three separate traditions: cattle, oil, and Indians. This was the Indian Territory, after all, and it's a rare native Oklahoman who doesn't have some Indian blood in his veins.

Oil wells ring the lawn of the Capitol Building in Oklahoma City, a metropolis of nearly a million people. The stockyards here are the world's busiest, and the city's National Cowboy Hall of Fame and Western Heritage Center offers the world's most extensive collection of western lore (including John Wayne's collection of Pueblo kachina dolls).

Tulsa is an attractive cosmopolitan city and Oklahoma's cultural center, with museums, a fine symphony orchestra, and theater, opera, and dance companies.

Rodeos and ranches, gypsum caves and wildlife refuges, the Tom Mix, Will Rogers, and Pawnee Bill Museums—Oklahoma is still as full of the Wild West spirit as it was when the first homesteaders rushed to claim their piece of it.

As far as elephant-eye-high corn goes, it hardly matters that even little Delaware produces nearly twice as many bushels: Oklahoma is still O.K.

Oklahoma
THE SOONER STATE

TULSA POWWOW, MOHAWK PARK

ALABASTER CAVERNS STATE PARK, NEAR FREEDOM

THE STATE CAPITOL, OKLAHOMA CITY

EIGHTY-NINER DAY CELEBRATION, GUTHRIE

PECAN FESTIVAL, OKMULGEE

THE CHEROKEE HERITAGE CENTER, TAHLEQUAH

ORIGIN OF NAME
From two Choctaw Indian words meaning "red people"

CAPITAL
Oklahoma City

STATE FLOWER
Mistletoe

STATE BIRD
Scissortailed Flycatcher

YEAR OF STATEHOOD
1907 (46th state)

FAMOUS OKLAHOMANS
Carl Albert, Johnny Bench, James Garner, Woody Guthrie, Mickey Mantle, Reba McEntire, Carry Nation, Wiley Post, Oral Roberts, Will Rogers, Jim Thorpe

THE MITTENS, MONUMENT VALLEY, ARIZONA

The West

Washington
THE EVERGREEN STATE

Most of Washington's population is clustered around Puget Sound, which, with 2000 miles of shoreline, is one of the world's great inland waterways.

Seattle, perched on the Sound and backed with mighty Mount Rainier, typifies the state's unique marriage of natural beauty and urban sophistication. The city began to boom when gold was discovered in the Klondike, and the opening of the Panama Canal further stimulated its growth. Here, the futuristic Space Needle from the 1962 World's Fair coexists easily with the Pike Place Market, the oldest continuously operated farmer's market in the country.

On the other side of the state is Spokane, the largest rail center west of Omaha and heart of the rich "Inland Empire," which produces 85 percent of America's dried peas, 80 percent of its hops, 35 percent of its apples, and 25 percent of its white wheat.

There are plenty of other interesting places in between. Grand Coulee Dam is the world's largest hydroelectric facility. The wild San Juan Islands are home to soaring bald eagles. Omak is the baby's breath capital of the world. The 28 miles of seashore at Long Beach is one of the longest hard sand beaches in the world. Mount Rainier National Park's 26 major glaciers hold more ice than all the glaciers in the rest of the country (except Alaska) put together.

No discussion of Washington would be complete without a word about the weather. Because the Cascade Mountains hurl back the moisture from the Pacific Ocean, some of the wettest and the driest areas of the nation are only a mountain range away. Inland Washington receives an average of 15 inches of rainfall a year, compared to 135 inches on the Olympic Peninsula, where rain forests grow. And the heaviest snowfall ever recorded in the United States fell on Mount Rainier's Paradise Glacier in 1971/72. How would you like to wake up one morning and face shoveling 93 feet of snow?

MT. SHUKSAN, NORTHWESTERN WASHINGTON

SEATTLE

ORIGIN OF NAME
After George Washington

CAPITAL
Olympia

STATE FLOWER
Western Rhododendron

STATE BIRD
Willow Goldfinch

YEAR OF STATEHOOD
1889 (42nd state)

FAMOUS WASHINGTONIANS
Bing Crosby, William O. Douglas,
Henry M. Jackson, Gary Larson,
Mary McCarthy

156

MT. ST. HELENS, SOUTHWESTERN WASHINGTON

SUQUAMISH TRIBAL MUSEUM, SUQUAMISH

WESTERN WASHINGTON FAIR, PUYALLUP

ICE CAVES, RANIER NATIONAL PARK

FT. VANCOUVER, VANCOUVER

The popular conception of the Southwest is so dominated by deserts that Arizona's pine forests, fertile valleys, mountains, and rolling rangeland are liable to come as a surprise.

There is desert here, of course—plenty of it. This is a state where they have national monuments for sandstone formations, petrified forests, and different varieties of cactus. The colors of the Painted Desert have inspired a generation of designers and artists.

There are also Indians: Arizona has the largest native American population of any state. More than 14 tribes are represented on 20 reservations, including huge Hopi and Navajo territories.

In recent years this last of the 48 contiguous states has become one of the most popular places in America to relocate, retire, or just plain visit.

Phoenix, rising on the ruins of an ancient Hohokam Indian settlement like the fabled Egyptian bird for which it is named, is the 10th-largest city in the nation and the cultural center of the Southwest. Tucson, once a small Spanish mission town, has become a major sunbelt resort area. The mountain city of Flagstaff offers skiing, and at Four Corners Monument in Teec Nos Pos, visitors can stand in Arizona, New Mexico, Utah, and Colorado at the same time.

Nothing that man will ever make, however, can compare to the astonishing mile-deep Grand Canyon, cut over millenia by the winding Colorado River. More than 4 million visitors each year marvel at nature's spectacular handiwork.

Finally, let's not forget that little piece of the Old West known as Tombstone, where the Earp Brothers and "Doc" Holliday gunned it out with the Clantons and McLaurys at the O. K. Corral. Plenty of gunfighters are buried in Tombstone's cemetery, Boot Hill. One gravestone reads, "Here lies Lester Moore/Shot to death with a .44/No Les, no more."

APACHE TRIBAL CEREMONY

TUCSON

Arizona
THE GRAND CANYON STATE

159

GRAND CANYON

TUCSON GEM AND MINERAL SHOW

PRESCOTT RODEO

THE PAINTED DESERT, PETRIFIED FOREST NATIONAL PARK

FOURTH AVENUE STREET FAIR, TUCSON

SAILING, LAKE HAVASU

WHITE HOUSE RUIN, CANYON DE CHELLY NATIONAL MONUMENT

MEXICAN FIESTA, TUCSON

ORIGIN OF NAME
From Pima Indian word "arizonac," meaning "little spring of water"

CAPITAL
Phoenix

STATE FLOWER
Flower of the Saguaro Cactus

STATE BIRD
Cactus Wren

YEAR OF STATEHOOD
1912 (48th state)

FAMOUS ARIZONANS
Cochise, Geronimo, Barry Goldwater, Zane Grey, George W. P. Hunt, Helen Jacobs, Percival Lowell, Morris and Stewart Udall

Critics called the 1867 purchase of Alaska from Russia "Seward's Folly," after Secretary of State William Seward who negotiated the deal. The price was $7.2 million—about 2 cents per acre for land that turned out to be not only some of the most beautiful in the world but rich in gold, oil, and other resources as well.

Alaska is the land of superlatives. It is the largest state—twice the size of the closest runner-up, Texas, and bigger than England, France, Spain, and Italy combined. It is the most western state—on the same longitude as New Zealand. It has the tallest mountain (the 20,306-foot Mount McKinley), the most wildlife, and both the shortest and longest days, depending on what time of the year you visit (in Barrow, 800 miles from the North Pole, the sun doesn't set at all in the summer, and in the winter it doesn't rise for two full months). Its shoreline (33,904 miles) is greater than the rest of America's coastline combined.

No wonder Alaskans are tough, independent, and proud; it takes a unique combination of self-sufficiency, teamwork, good humor, and humility to survive in the "Land of the Midnight Sun."

Practically everything else you can say about Alaska involves some statistic or event that would rate at least a "gee whiz" anywhere else.

More than half the state's population—about 250,000—lives in Anchorage, where the strongest earthquake ever recorded in North America struck on Good Friday, 1964. Ketchikan, the southernmost city in the state, receives an incredible 164 inches of rainfall annually. In 1971, Prospect Creek recorded America's coldest temperature: 80 degrees below zero. And, perhaps most mind-boggling of all, not only has Alaska no income tax, but oil revenues actually allow the state to pay dividends to its residents!

Alaska

THE LAST FRONTIER

MT. MCKINLEY NATIONAL PARK,
SOUTH CENTRAL ALASKA

CRUISE SHIP IN GLACIER BAY

ANCHORAGE

TLINGET INDIANS, HAINES

CHILKAT NATIVE CRAFTS

CHILKAT DANCERS, JUNEAU

ESKIMO CHILD

ORIGIN OF NAME
From the Aleut Indian word
"Alashka," meaning the "Great Land"

CAPITAL
Juneau

STATE FLOWER
Forget-me-not

STATE BIRD
Willow Ptarmigan

YEAR OF STATEHOOD
1959 (49th state)

FAMOUS ALASKANS
Tom Bodett, Susan Butcher, Carl
Eielson, Ernest Gruening, Joe
Juneau, Sydney Laurence, James
Wickersham

FISHER TOWERS, GRAND COUNTY

Utah

THE BEEHIVE STATE

Though it was visited by Spanish missionaries and American trappers, Utah remained a rugged, unsettled wilderness until a small band of men and women, hardened by adversity and possessing a strength greater than themselves, traveled down Emigration Canyon to the Salt Lake Valley.

"This is the place," said Brigham Young, of the alkaline wasteland deemed unfit for human habitation by Indians and explorers. The Great Salt Lake was the saltiest body of water on earth after the Dead Sea, but its shores bloomed, thanks to the faith and determination of Young's followers, the members of the Church of Jesus Christ of Latter-day Saints (the Mormons).

Other Mormons followed—thousands making the journey west by pushing handcarts the 1300 miles from the church's base in Illinois—and today the population of Utah is 70 percent Mormon. Great cities like Provo and Salt Lake City stand as testimony to the courage of these pioneers.

Utah is hardly tamed, however. The land itself is forever wild, beautiful, unique. With the Rockies to the east, the Great Basin stretching to Nevada's mountains to the west, and dramatic canyons that culminate in the Grand Canyon to the south, Utah has an abundance of natural riches.

There are six national forests, five national parks, and six national monuments in the state. Rainbow Bridge is so immense that the Capitol dome in Washington, D.C., could fit beneath it. Canyonlands National Park is filled with fantastic mesas and natural formations. Arches National Park has the greatest concentration of natural stone arches in the world.

Bryce Canyon National Park is a natural wonderland of cliffs, spires, and pinnacles with names like Fairy Castle, Wall of Windows, and The Alligator. Said Ebenezer Bryce, a Mormon rancher who gave the place its name: "It's a hell of a place to lose a cow."

THE TEMPLE SQUARE ASSEMBLY HALL, SALT LAKE CITY

167

THE TEMPLE OF OSIRIS, BRYCE CANYON

GRAVEYARD, GRAFTON

NAVAJO INDIANS, MONUMENT VALLEY

MORMON CHURCH, SPRING CITY

THE SALT LAKE TABERNACLE, SALT LAKE CITY

ORIGIN OF NAME
From the Ute tribe, meaning "people of the mountains"

CAPITAL
Salt Lake City

STATE FLOWER
Sego Lily

STATE BIRD
Seagull

YEAR OF STATEHOOD
1896 (45th state)

FAMOUS UTAHANS
Maude Adams, J. Willard Marriott, the Osmond Family, Merlin Olsen, George Romney, Brigham Young, Loretta Young

The fabulous rocky coastline, the vast tracts of timber (the nation's largest standing reserve), and the mighty Cascade Mountains give the impression that the Oregon wilderness could only be tamed by lumberjacks and mountain men.

In fact, much of the state is gentle country dotted with small towns and covered bridges reminiscent of New England and the Midwest, from where the pioneers of the 1840s who settled Oregon had set out. The fertile Willamette Valley at the end of the Oregon Trail was everything these farmers had prayed for during the long crossing.

Portland, in the shadow of mammoth Mount Hood, is the state's largest city. Full of parks and fountains, it is known as the City of Roses because of its gardens and festival. The city's Yamhill Historic District has the most cast-iron buildings in the nation. More Asian elephants are bred at the city's Washington Park Zoo than anywhere outside the Orient.

Venture outside the big city, however, and you find some surprises. Some of the best wines outside of California are being made in the hills near McMinnville and Newberg. This area is also responsible for 90 percent of America's hazelnuts. Ashland has a renowned Shakespeare Festival. Salem and sophisticated Eugene are alive with history and festivals. Perhaps the finest maritime museum in the West can be found in Astoria, which John Jacob Astor's partners sailed around Cape Horn to found in 1811. The beautiful Coos Bay is the world's largest shipping port for forest products.

Still, the haunting beauty of rivers, mountains, and forests, and natural marvels like the impossibly blue Crater Lake (America's deepest) leave no heart untouched. No wonder Americans have been flocking to Oregon since two tourists named Lewis and Clark arrived here in 1805.

CALIFORNIA STREET, JACKSONVILLE

PORTLAND

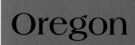

Oregon
THE BEAVER STATE

BEACH NEAR NESKOWIN

MT. JEFFERSON, NEAR SALEM

FARMLAND, NEAR BAKER

SAND CASTLE CONTEST, CANNON BEACH

SHAKESPEARE FESTIVAL, ASHLAND

THE PORTLAND BUILDING

ORIGIN OF NAME
Unknown

CAPITAL
Salem

STATE FLOWER
Oregon Grape

STATE BIRD
Western Meadowlark

YEAR OF STATEHOOD
1859 (33rd state)

FAMOUS OREGONIANS
Mel Blanc, Ernest Bloch, Raymond Carver, Chief Joseph, Edwin Markham, Joaquin Miller, Linus Pauling, John Reed, Alberto Salazar, "Doc" Severinsen

DESERT PLANT, CARLSBAD CAVERN
NATIONAL PARK

MARIACHI BAND, SANTA FE FESTIVAL

FRUIT STAND, VELARDE

A unique blend of Hispanic, pioneer, and Native American cultures has flourished amid the spellbinding vistas of New Mexico, a land of stark deserts and alpine meadows, majestic mountains and rolling grassland, endless horizons, and limestone caves.

Perhaps no place better exemplifies New Mexico's mystery and romance than Sante Fe. Spain's provincial capital a decade before the Pilgrims landed at Plymouth Rock, Sante Fe today is a unique community full of culture and verve. The city is home to extraordinary museums, historic buildings (the Palace for Governors is the oldest public building in the United States), the third-largest art market in the world, and the world-renowned Sante Fe Opera.

Booming Albuquerque, where a third of the state's population resides, is one of the oldest cities in the United States and at the same time one of the youngest—the average age of its residents is only 28.

Art is big business in exotic Taos, a town of less than 5000, with more than 60 galleries. The Carlsbad Caverns, east of the Sacramento Mountains, are the largest underground network of caves in the world. In the dry canyons of the state you can see the abandoned cliff dwellings of the Anasazi Indians, who resided in five-story apartments when most Europeans were living in huts. A sea of gypsum stretches for miles in White Sands National Monument. Farther north is the site of the world's first atomic explosion.

Fittingly, this peaceful, quiet state is the final resting place for several famous individuals. The ashes of D. H. Lawrence are enshrined outside of Taos; Billy the Kid is buried in Fort Sumner; and interred at Capitan are the remains of a very important bear, who as a cub was rescued from a forest fire. That's right. They called him "Smokey."

THE SANTA FE OPERA

SANDIA TRAMWAY, ALBUQUERQUE

New Mexico
LAND OF ENCHANTMENT

INDIAN MARKET, SANTA FE

13TH-CENTURY RUINS,
GILA CLIFF DWELLINGS NATIONAL MONUMENT,
SOUTHWEST NEW MEXICO

ORIGIN OF NAME
The territory (along with Arizona)
was ceded to the United States by
Mexico after the War of 1848

CAPITAL
Santa Fe

STATE FLOWER
Yucca

STATE BIRD
Roadrunner

YEAR OF STATEHOOD
1912 (47th state)

FAMOUS NEW MEXICANS
William H. Bonney, Nancy Lopez,
Bill Mauldin, Georgia O'Keeffe,
Kim Stanley, Al and Bobby Unser

SAN MIGUEL MISSION, SANTA FE

Hawaii

THE ALOHA STATE

The newest state, Hawaii, is actually a 1600-mile mountain range, an archipelago of volcanoes that began rising from the depths of the Pacific Ocean 40 million years ago. Today, 132 such mountaintops stand above the tide, forming what Mark Twain called "the loveliest fleet of islands anchored in any sea."

Of the five major islands, Oahu is the most familiar to mainlanders. It was here on December 7, 1941, that a surprise attack decimated America's Pacific Fleet. Today, Oahu is a busy tropical paradise. Honolulu is home to some 380,000 Americans and the site of such familiar places as Diamond Head and Waikiki Beach, and the somber U.S.S. *Arizona* National Memorial in Pearl Harbor.

Volcanoes National Park on the "Big Island" of Hawaii is a naturalist's dream. Mauna Kea and Mauna Loa (the world's most massive mountain) are the stars here, both nearly 14,000 feet in height (30,000 from the ocean floor).

Kauai is the "Garden Island," a lush place of sugarcane plantations and ancient eroded craters—the slopes of Waialeale may be the wettest spot on earth. Kauai was the movie location of Bali Ha'i in the movie of *South Pacific*.

Maui, the second largest island, is dominated by elegant resorts and the 10,023-foot Haleakala, the world's largest dormant volcano. As many as 400 whaling ships at a time once anchored off her shores. The islands of Molokai and Lanai are chiefly devoted to agriculture, but each, too, has its charms.

And there is good news for the more than 1 million tourists who come to Hawaii each year: only a brief 10,000 years from now, Lo'ihi, the newest Hawaiian island, is scheduled to rise from the sea.

OUTRIGGER AND WINDSURFER, KIHEI

DIAMOND HEAD AND WAIKIKI BEACH, HONOLULU

HANALEI VALLEY, KAUAI

THE POLYNESIAN CULTURAL CENTER, LAIE

THE U.S.S. *ARIZONA* MEMORIAL, HONOLULU

GIRLS WEARING LEIS, WAILEA

ORIGIN OF NAME
Possibly after their traditional discoverer, Hawaii Loa, or perhaps after "Hawaiki," the native word for homeland

CAPITAL
Honolulu

STATE FLOWER
Yellow Hibiscus

STATE BIRD
Nene (Hawaiian Goose)

YEAR OF STATEHOOD
1959 (50th state)

FAMOUS ISLANDERS
Bette Midler, John A. Burns, Father Damien de Veuster, Don Ho, Daniel K. Inouye, King Kamehameha, Queen Kaahumanu, Queen Liliuokalani, Ellison Onizuka

OAHU

Wyoming

THE EQUALITY STATE

What do the terms "wide open spaces" and "elbow room" really mean? Well, let's put it this way: in Manhattan there are 64,922 people per square mile; in Wyoming there are 5.

Casper, the hub of the Rocky Mountain's oil and gas industry, is Wyoming's largest city with a population of only 51,000. Cheyenne, with a few thousand less, is next, though the town doubles in size each July during Cheyenne Frontier Days— the world's oldest and largest rodeo. Buffalo Bill interviewed hopeful cowboys on the porch of the inn in Sheridan before he founded his own hotel—the Irma, named after his youngest daughter—in his own town, Cody. The cherrywood back bar (that some claim Queen Victoria gave the old showman) can still be seen there.

But why are we talking about cities when the scenery here is so fabulous? People come from all over the world to ski the legendary slopes at Jackson Hole; to see the world's largest mineral hot spring at Thermopolis and the stark looming Devil's Tower (the country's first national monument); to experience the glorious Grand Tetons and the wonders of America's first national park, Yellowstone.

Within the 3472 square miles of Yellowstone are a waterfall twice as high as Niagara; a large population of bison, moose, elk, bighorn sheep, and bears; black obsidian cliffs, from which the native Indians made arrowheads they traded to tribes as far away as Ohio; and, of course, the unique hydrothermal activity that sends boiling water spewing regularly from geysers like "Old Faithful."

Why do they call it the "Equality State"? Apparently the tough cowboys here have always known which side their skillet bread was buttered on: Wyoming was the first state to grant women the vote, the first to have a woman justice of the peace, the first to let women serve as jurors, and the first to elect a woman governor.

SQUARE TOP MOUNTAIN, WIND RIVER MOUNTAIN RANGE

FRONTIER DAYS, CHEYENNE

ORIGIN OF NAME
From the Algonquin *mache-weaming*—"at the big flats"

CAPITAL
Cheyenne

STATE FLOWER
Indian Paintbrush

STATE BIRD
Meadowlark

YEAR OF STATEHOOD
1890 (44th state)

FAMOUS WYOMINGITES
James Bridger, Curt Gowdy, Nellie Tayloe Ross

MAMMOTH HOT SPRINGS, YELLOWSTONE NATIONAL PARK

OLD FAITHFUL, YELLOWSTONE NATIONAL PARK

SHOSHONE INDIANS, WIND RIVER INDIAN RESERVATION

OLD TRAIL TOWN, CODY

OFFICERS' DEN, FORT BRIDGER STATE HISTORICAL CENTER, NEAR EVANSTON

HOT AIR BALLOON RALLY, NEAR RIVERTON

NEVADA DAY PARADE, CARSON CITY

LAS VEGAS

Nevada means Las Vegas to most people—a city that was virtually nonexistent until 1931, when the state legalized gambling. Today, Vegas receives more than 18 million visitors each year, and they don't come just for the entertainment extravaganzas, the 50-cent shrimp cocktails, or even the Liberace Museum; those one-armed bandits and roulette wheels hum to the tune of more than $2 billion annually.

Even Reno, surrounded by the gorgeous scenery of Lake Tahoe (which has one of the greatest concentrations of ski lifts in the world), and a place clever enough to make divorce into a major industry, depends upon the casinos to keep it the "Biggest Little City in the World."

While we may think of Nevada in terms of neon, glitter, and gambling, most of the state is eerily beautiful desert, thanks to the towering Sierra Nevadas which cut off any flow of moisture from the Pacific.

Nevada's history has been tied to its mineral wealth since the discovery of the legendary Comstock Lode in Virginia City in 1859. This rich silver deposit prompted Abraham Lincoln to push for the admittance of Nevada into the Union to help finance the Civil War.

Though it is the driest state (only 3.73 inches of rain each year), the 115-mile Lake Mead is the largest man-made body of water in America. The mighty Hoover Dam, which created the lake, contains enough concrete to pave a highway 16 feet wide from New York to San Francisco.

How far does the rest of Nevada really diverge from the Las Vegas image? Let's put it this way: the state has a substantial population of Basques who preserve the customs and culture of their native Pyrenees Mountains. When was the last time Wayne Newton yodeled that traditional piercing Basque war cry, an *irrintzi*?

Nevada

**THE SAGEBRUSH STATE
THE SILVER STATE**

CATHEDRAL GORGE STATE PARK

HOOVER DAM, LAKE MEAD NATIONAL RECREATION AREA

PIPER'S OPERA HOUSE, VIRGINIA CITY

ORIGIN OF NAME
Spanish for "snow-capped"

CAPITAL
Carson City

STATE FLOWER
Sagebrush

STATE BIRD
Mountain Bluebird

YEAR OF STATEHOOD
1864 (36th state)

FAMOUS NEVADANS
Walter Van Tilburg Clark, Paul
Laxalt, John William Mackay, Pat
McCarran, Key Pittman, William
Morris Stewart

RENO

LAKE TAHOE

Idaho

THE GEM STATE

Although it is one of the fastest growing states in the nation, Idaho still has more than enough natural beauty and unpretentious hospitality to go around.

Rugged mountains dominate the north of the state, while both rich farmlands and deserts can be found to the south. More than 40 percent of Idaho is preserved in national forests and wilderness areas, but unique sights are everywhere.

Hell's Canyon, cut nearly 8000 feet into the earth by the winding Snake River, is the deepest gorge in North America. The longest river in any state, the Salmon is called the "River of No Return" because the swift current and steep canyons give rafters no chance of turning back. The 83 square miles of volcanic landscapes in Craters of the Moon National Monument are so otherworldly that our lunar astronauts trained there.

National Geographic has called the crystal-clear Lake Coeur d'Alene one of the most beautiful in the world. Just east of there are the richest silver mines in the country. Eight-hundred-year-old cedars, 12 feet across and 150 feet tall, grow in the Roosevelt Grove near pristine Priest Lake. Sun Valley, the nation's first ski resort, still offers some of the best skiing in the United States, and throughout Idaho the salmon and trout fishing is superb.

The outdoor lifestyle has always attracted self-sufficient people here, including Ernest Hemingway. The Basques came for the sheepherding near Boise, and there are now more of them in Idaho than anywhere outside the European Pyrenees. Others came to farm. Agriculture is the state's chief industry.

How many of those famous potatoes does Idaho produce each year? Enough for you to go to your local McDonald's and get 53 million orders of fries, that's all.

INDIAN EXPO, BOISE

THE SNAKE RIVER, NEAR BOISE

THE SAWTOOTH MOUNTAINS, NEAR STANLEY

STATE CAPITAL, BOISE

WILDFLOWER FIELD, SAWTOOTH WILDERNESS

JAIALDI, BOISE

PIERRE'S HOLE RENDEZVOUS, DRIGGS

ORIGIN OF NAME
Not really a Shoshone Indian word meaning "gem of the mountains," although it makes a nice story; perhaps a Kiowa Apache term for the Commanches

CAPITAL
Boise

STATE FLOWER
Syringa

STATE BIRD
Mountain Bluebird

YEAR OF STATEHOOD
1890 (43rd state)

FAMOUS IDAHOANS
William E. Borah, Frank Church, Fred T. Dubois, Philo Farnsworth, Barbara Morgan, Sacagawea, Lana Turner

SUN VALLEY

ICE SCULPTURE, McCALL

LOS ANGELES

California
THE GOLDEN STATE

If California seems to be all things to all people, perhaps it is because this is where you can see 30-story-tall trees that were centuries old when Moses led the Israelites out of Egypt; where you can find the highest and lowest places in the contiguous 48 states (Death Valley and Mount Whitney); where everything from miraculous wine to silicon chips are made; and where everyone from Richard Nixon to Mickey Mouse was born.

California is the most populous state and in many ways the most diverse. The scenery ranges from pristine beaches and spectacular mountains to fertile valleys and austere deserts. The choices of lifestyle are bounded only by the imagination of the same folks that make the movies.

To begin with, there's the laid-back crazy quilt of freeway culture, ethnic influences, and glitz known as Los Angeles. L.A. seems more like a dozen cities than one. Hollywood, Beverly Hills, Malibu, Santa Monica, Pasadena . . . will the real Los Angeles stand up, please? Fer shure.

San Francisco, with its cable cars, Victorian houses (some 14,000 of them), and easygoing people, is one of the most enchanting towns in America. The awesome Golden Gate Bridge and the spectacular bay almost make Alcatraz on its rocky island look charming.

There's lovely San Diego with its world-famous zoo and, in Balboa Park, the largest concentration of museums in America, after the National Mall in Washington, D.C. In Long Beach, you can see the ocean liner *Queen Mary*, as well as Howard Hughes's flying behemoth, the "Spruce Goose." The untamed coast of Big Sur thrills all that pass on their way to the fabulous Hearst castle, San Simeon.

What wonders have we left out? Only Disneyland, Lake Tahoe, Palm Springs, Santa Barbara, Monterey, and a national park the size of Rhode Island called Yosemite—to name just a handful.

LOMBARD STREET, SAN FRANCISCO

THE HEARST SAN SIMEON HISTORICAL MONUMENT

SEQUOIA NATIONAL PARK

SUNBATHING, SANTA CRUZ

CHINESE CHESS, SAN FRANCISCO

RODEO DRIVE, BEVERLY HILLS

ORIGIN OF NAME
After an imaginary earthly paradise in Garcia Ordóñez de Montalvo's 1510 romance, *Las Serges de Esplandian*

CAPITAL
Sacramento

STATE FLOWER
Golden Poppy

STATE BIRD
California Valley Quail

YEAR OF STATEHOOD
1850 (31st state)

FAMOUS CALIFORNIANS
Luther Burbank, John C. Frémont, Bret Harte, Jack London, Aimee Semple McPherson, John Muir, Richard M. Nixon, William Saroyan, John Steinbeck, Earl Warren

STEINER STREET, SAN FRANCISCO

MANN'S CHINESE THEATRE, LOS ANGELES

THE GOLDEN GATE BRIDGE, SAN FRANCISCO

COASTLINE NEAR SANTA BARBARA

DISNEYLAND, ANAHEIM

YELLOWSTONE FALLS, YOSEMITE NATIONAL PARK

Alaska, Texas, and California are larger in area, but Montana doesn't need to be the biggest at anything —or the oldest, or the first. Big Sky Country doesn't need to prove itself. It simply is.

Cattle now graze where millions of buffalo once roamed across the great prairies of the eastern two thirds of the state. Ranches 100 square miles in size are not un- known. In the west, the Rockies rise in blue-green majesty—"the land of shining mountains," the Indians called it.

Billings, Montana's largest city, with a population of only about 80,000, is not far from the battlefield where Col. George Armstrong Custer and his troops were wiped out by an overwhelming force of Sioux and Cheyenne. Virginia City and Helena owe their existence to the state's vast mineral wealth; both were booming gold towns, while the region around Butte and Anaconda has supplied much of the country's copper.

The state's most magnificent trea- sures, however, are available for all to see in Glacier National Park, a million pristine acres of towering peaks and evergreen forests. Here you can drive across the Continen- tal Divide on Going-to-the-Sun Road and see alpine meadows ablaze with wildflowers, hundreds of ice-blue lakes, and dozens of glaciers.

Montana's spirit and history were perhaps best captured by Charles M. Russell, the internationally acclaimed "cowboy artist." His paintings of Native Americans and of the great vanished buffalo herds, like his canvas *When the Land Be- longed to God*, can be seen in museums all across the state.

"My brother," said Russell with the hospitality of a true Montanan, "when you come to my lodge, the robe will be spread and the pipe of peace will be lit."

Montana
THE TREASURE STATE

BILLINGS

FESTIVAL OF THE NATIONS, RED LODGE

MT. SINOPAH, GLACIER NATIONAL PARK

MOUNTAIN GOAT, GLACIER NATIONAL PARK

ORIGIN OF NAME
Latin or Spanish for "mountainous"

CAPITAL
Helena

STATE FLOWER
Bitterroot

STATE BIRD
Western Meadowlark

YEAR OF STATEHOOD
1889 (41st state)

FAMOUS MONTANANS
Gary Cooper, Chet Huntley, Myrna
Loy, Mike Mansfield, Brent
Musberger, Charles M. Russell,
Lester Thurow

YOUNG COWBOY, HOLLAND LAKE LODGE

THE GRANT-KOHRS RANCH NATIONAL HISTORIC SITE, DEER LODGE

LOGGER DAYS, KALISPELL

DENVER

CITY AND COUNTY BUILDING, DENVER

SKIING, NEW DENVER

The eastern third of Colorado is a sagebrush desert plain which suddenly erupts into America's highest mountains, the Rockies. Some 1000 peaks top 10,000 feet and 54 exceed 14,000 feet.

Highly developed irrigation systems have made Colorado rich in agriculture; miners have long exploited the state's abundant natural resources, and manufacturing now provides thousands of jobs. But with scenery like this, it's not surprising that tourism is the number one industry.

Over half the state's population lives in the mile-high metropolis of Denver, at the foot of the Rockies. One of the fastest-growing cities in the country, Denver gets nearly 300 days of sun each year and boasts more sporting goods stores per capita than anywhere else in the world.

The U.S. Air Force Academy is located in Colorado Springs; in Golden you can tour the Coors brewery (the world's largest); there are gargantuan sand dunes in the San Luis Valley and Anasazi cliff dwellings in Mesa Verde National Park.

Still, it is the Rockies that dominate Colorado, and the best way to enjoy these wonderful mountains is just to drive through them.

Check out the ski resorts of Vail, Steamboat Springs. and Aspen, which is a magnet for the "beautiful people" even in the summer, thanks to its music festivals, boutiques, and restaurants. Sally out into Rocky Mountain National Park from picturesque towns like Grand Lake and Estes Park. Take the Pikes Peak Highway and see the view from the 14,110-foot summit that inspired Katharine Lee Bates in 1893 to write the words to "America the Beautiful."

Perhaps your Colorado experience will make you agree with Teddy Roosevelt's description of Cripple Creek's Gold Camp Road: "The trip that bankrupts the English language."

Colorado

CENTENNIAL STATE

ORIGIN OF NAME
Spanish for "red"; first applied to
the Colorado River

CAPITAL
Denver

STATE FLOWER
Rocky Mountain Columbine

STATE BIRD
Lark Bunting

YEAR OF STATEHOOD
1876 (38th state)

FAMOUS COLORADANS
Molly Brown, William N. Byers,
M. Scott Carpenter, Jack Dempsey,
John Denver, Douglas Fairbanks, Jr.,
Lowell Thomas, Byron R. White,
Paul Whiteman

RODEO, MONTE VISTA

RAFTING, COLORADO RIVER

GEORGETOWN

THE MOLLY BROWN HOUSE, DENVER

OKTOBERFEST, DENVER

THE GARDEN OF THE GODS, COLORADO SPRINGS

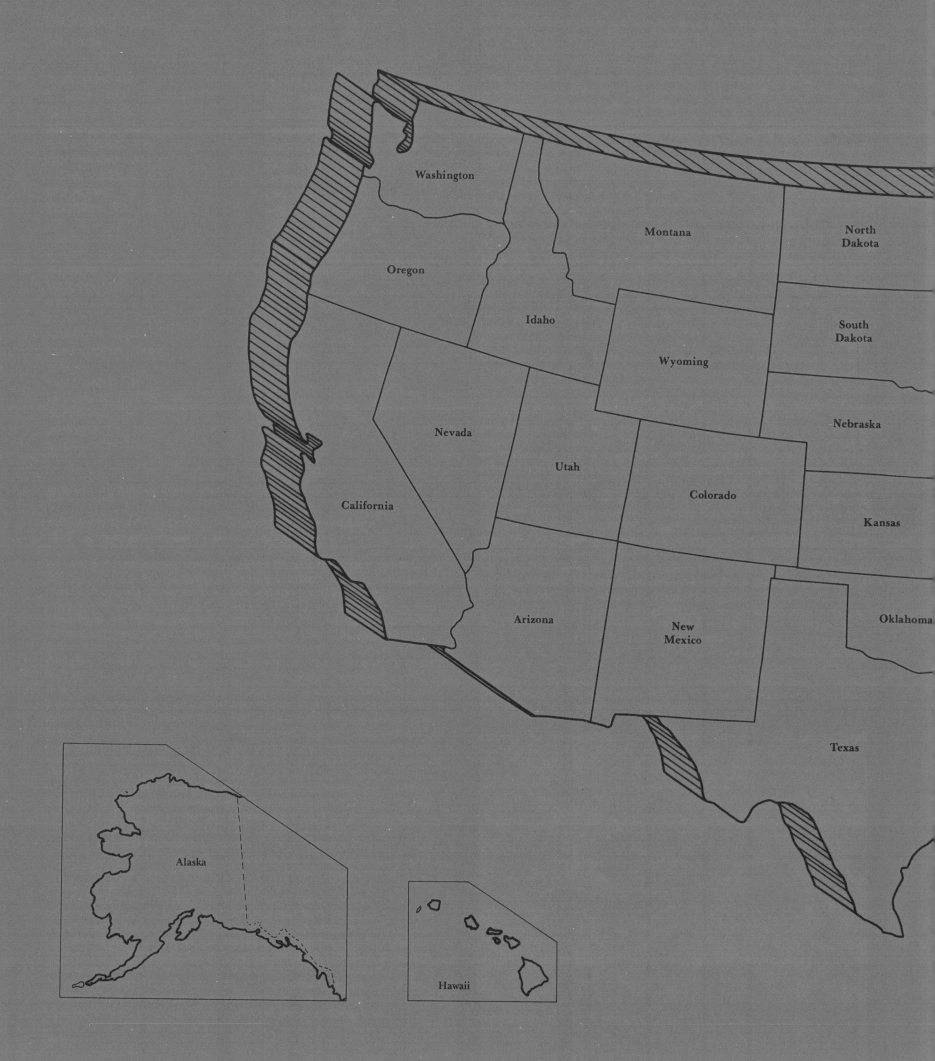